Sunnyvale, Ca. 94087

SAN FRANCISCO

IN A TEACUP

San Francisco in a Teacup

a guidebook for tea lovers

Fifty Unique Places to Have Tea in San Francisco and the Bay Area

Ulrica Hume

BLUE
CIRCLE
PRESS
™

SAN FRANCISCO IN A TEACUP

Copyright © 1999 by Ulrica Hume
All rights reserved.

❦

Publisher's Cataloging-in-Publication
(Provided by Quality Books, Inc.)

Hume, Ulrica.
San Francisco in a teacup : a guidebook for tea
lovers : fifty unique places to have tea in San
Francisco and the Bay Area / Ulrica Hume. — 1st ed.
p. cm.
Includes bibliographical references and index.
LCCN: 98-94895
ISBN: 0-9669193-0-0

1. Tearooms — California — San Francisco Bay Area
— Guidebooks. 2. San Francisco Bay Area —
Guidebooks. I. Title.

TX907.3.C22S3692 1999
647.95'794'6
QBI98-1749

❦

Blue Circle Press
P.O. Box 460055
San Francisco, CA 94146

ORDERING INFORMATION
See order form at back of book (page 224).
Inquiries and orders, contact the address above,
send tea-mail to uhume@compuserve.com
or visit our web site at http://www.bluecirclepress.com

First Edition — 1999
Printed in the United States of America

BOOK DESIGN BY SCRIBEWORKS™

MAPS ILLUSTRATED BY ULRICA HUME

COMPUTER WIZARDRY BY MICHAEL GRAZIANO

*"Teacups" cover art (artist unknown, England, circa 1895)
reprinted with the kind permission of Cavallini & Co., San Francisco.*

Thank You...

THIS BOOK IS DEDICATED TO THE SPIRIT OF TEA

Michael Graziano,
Peter Nasmyth, and
Julie Novak-McSweeney.

Roy Fong, Helen Gustafson,
Molly Klupfell, Sarah Meakin,
James Norwood Pratt, and
Kathi Wong for inspiration and guidance along the way of tea.

Curt & Vickie Hume, David Joseph, Frank Miraglia, Shirley
Read-Jahn, and Liz Sizensky. Jennie Bayer, Bob Greenebaum, Jeff
Kause, Kerwin Leader of McNaughton & Gunn. Patricia Akre
and Selby Collins of the San Francisco History Center, and the
telephone reference staff of the San Francisco New Main Library.

Thanks also to Jeff Bacon, Norman Barahona & Jena Rose, Christy
Bartlett, Andrew Campbell, Timothy Castle, David Furukawa
Chen, Phyllis Christopher, Frederic Clark, Mary Claire Draeger
DeSoto, David Egert, Ph.D., Pamela Forbes, Robyn Scott & Betty
Forbes, Don George, Pilar Gutierrez, Terri Harte, Tricia
Hollenberg, Angela Jackson, Tessa Judd, Tom Keelan, Lucy Li,
Moon Ma, Mike Macadaan, Jon Makhmaltchi, Kim Maloof, Scott
McDougall, Valérie Miscot, Marsha Monro, Raina Moore,
Adrienne Morello, David Nemoyten, Megan Olson, Roberta
Oswald, Kristi Palmer, Brad Parberry, Diana Parker, Michael
Perricone, Renée Pestana, Herb Pierrepont & Karen Strange, Jill
Portman & Gary Shinner, Rand Richards, Byron Rudolph,
Betty Shelton, Rose Shoshana, Joseph Simrany, Douglas Smith,
Steven E. Steigman, Guy Stilson, Janet Toman, Barbara
Traisman, Amber Vierra, Bettina Vitell, Randall Weingarten,
Meiya Wender, David Wiener, Thomas Wolfe, Amanda Zucker,
Samara Zuwaylif, and to all the tearoom owners and staff for their
time and hospitality.

...and to the memory of my grandmothers, Sophie Huleva and
Amy Grace Hume.

TABLE OF CONTENTS

Illustrations   9

Introduction   11
*Why Tea?...The History of Tea...The Way
of Tea...How to Use this Book...A Word
(or Two) about Transport...Happy Sipping!*

T r a d i t i o n a l
Fairmont Hotel   29
Mark Hopkins Hotel   32
Neiman Marcus   35
Palace Hotel   37
Park Hyatt Hotel   42
Renaissance Stanford Court Hotel   46
Ritz-Carlton Hotel   49
St. Francis Hotel   53

C o z y
The Butler's Pantry   58
The English Rose   60
The Garden Grill   63
King George Hotel   66
Lady Pierrepont's   70
Lisa's Tea Treasures   73
Lovejoy's   76
Tal-y-Tara   81
The Village Green   84

O l d   W o r l d
Green Gulch Farm Zen Center   88
Imperial Tea Court   91
Japanese Tea Garden   95
Lucy's Tea House   99
Side by Side   103
Urasenke Foundation   105

N e w   W o r l d
A'Cuppa Tea   110
Tea & Company   113
Tea Time   116

Offbeat

Café Andrea	120
Chai of Larkspur	123
Chez Panisse	127
Elizabeth F. Gamble Garden Center	130
Mad Magda's	133
O Chamé	135
San Francisco Museum of Modern Art	138

Sip of Tea

Alfred Schilling	144
Barnes & Noble	146
Borders	148
Café Hana	150
California Palace of the Legion of Honor	152
Cinderella	154
De Young Museum	156
Draeger's Market Place	158
Grace Cathedral	161
Greens	163
I Love Chocolate	165
Just Desserts	167
Kowloon	170
La Nouvelle Patisserie	172
San Francisco Art Institute	174
Tan Tan Café	176
Tea-n-Crumpets	178

Tea Lovers' Resources 182
Associations • Books • Magazines and Newsletters • Protocol School • Tea Ceremony Classes, Workshops, and Celebrations • Tea Shops • Mail-Order Tea • Tea-Time Edibles • Teaware • Virtual Tea • Useful Phone Numbers

Index	212
Acknowledgments	213
Maps & Legend	214–216
Tea Notes	217–220

ILLUSTRATIONS

The Fairmont's Lobby Lounge, circa 1950 — page 28

The Palace's Garden Court, then...and now — pages 38 & 39

Teddy Bear Tea at the Park Hyatt — page 44

Afternoon Tea at The Ritz-Carlton — page 50

Tea for Two at The English Rose — page 61

King George Advertisement, circa 1914 — page 67

The Table is Set for Tea at Lovejoy's — page 77

The Magic Mirror — page 78

Tea House and Moon Bridge, Japanese Tea Garden, circa 1899 — page 97

Little Girl in Chinese Mandarin Costume, by Lewis Carroll, circa 1880 — page 102

Tea & Company — page 112

Chai of Larkspur — page 124

Caffe Museo / San Francisco Museum of Modern Art — page 139

Dancers Around the Doré Vase, de Young Museum, circa 1926 — page 155

Gustave Draeger and the Original San Francisco Store, 1931 — page 159

Maps of San Francisco & the Bay Area — pages 214 & 215

INTRODUCTION

Tea leaves come in a thousand different shapes: some look like the boots of a Tartar, some like the breast of a buffalo, some like clouds approaching from the mountains; some look like the rippling on the water caused by a breeze, some have a dull brown color and look like freshly ploughed soil covered with puddles after a heavy rainfall. All of these are good teas.

Lu Yü
Ch'a Ching, A.D. 780

WHY TEA?

I love its clear, gemlike colors. Its varied scents and flavors; its mystique...

Tea has always been a part of my life. As a child, I served imaginary tea and mudpies to unsuspecting dolls. One of my first jobs was as an herbal tea saleswoman. The time came when, seeking a more peaceful, less agitated existence, I parted ways with coffee. Cups of Earl Grey, green tea, and Lapsang Souchong gave this writer fuel and comfort and inspiration. Then, while I was living in London, I happened upon a whole new world of tea.

It occurred at a rendezvous at Nichols tearoom, an intimate corner of the Café Royale in Piccadilly. I don't remember the decor — except mirrors and lifelike gilt caryatids. The waiter approached and, in a dignified manner, set down a large, three-tiered silver tray.

I had never seen a scone before, or, for that matter, sandwiches without their crusts. And what was "clotted" cream? From that point on, my British friend turned into a guide, our meeting gathering an aura of discovery.

Since then, I have had many adventures in tea. The

following pages record my San Francisco tea journeys, all of them touched by quirkiness and unexpected enchantment. I have found many tearooms where, despite rumors to the contrary, service is *not* a lost art. In the luxury hotels, for instance, one is treated like a queen (or king), and emerges feeling pampered and soothed. In every tearoom, tea does its magic.

Tea is universal. It crosses the barriers of culture and class, uniting those with a common passion. Perhaps it is because tea is an affordable luxury. The mere act of sipping it helps restore the better, more civilized aspects of behavior. (Agnes Repplier once put it like this: "It has been well said that tea is suggestive of a thousand wants, from which spring the decencies and luxuries of civilization.") Everywhere I went, from the Top of the Mark, to the humblest hangout, I heard these words repeated: "Tea is the new coffee."

It was inevitable, I suppose, that during my search for the perfect "cuppa," I was occasionally led astray. The Hang Ah Tea Room, I learned, is not a tearoom at all, but rather a time-warped dim sum restaurant. Tart to Tart (where I had a butterfly palmier amidst mediocre decor), is deserving of mention if only for its odd hours—every day, 6:00 a.m.–2:00 a.m. And it seems that any ghosts have long since left The Beach Chalet near Ocean Beach, where, during the 1930s, sisters Hattie and Minnie Mooser once ran a tearoom.

THE HISTORY OF TEA is sweetened by curious legends. Emperor Shen Nung, known in China as the Divine Healer, Divine Husbandman, and Divine Cultivator, is credited with its discovery in 2737 B.C., when a few windblown *Camellia sinensis* leaves fell into his pot of boiling water and, by happenstance, the first brew was made.

Then there's the ascetic, Bodhidharma (a.k.a. Daruma), who came from India to China with the intention of contemplating the virtues of Buddha for nine years. Angry with himself for falling asleep during the third year, he cut off his eyelids and tossed them onto the ground beside him, where two fatigue-dispelling tea plants sprang up. Influenced by

In 1903, Arthur Gray addressed the dichotomy between coffee and tea:

Coffee suggests taverns, cafes, sailing vessels, yachts, boarding-houses by the riverside, and pessimism. Tea suggests optimism. Coffee is a tonic; tea, a comfort. Coffee is prose; tea is poetry. Whoever thinks of taking coffee into a sickroom? Who doesn't think of taking in the comforting cup of tea? Can the most vivid imagination picture the angels above the stars drinking coffee? No. Yet, if I were to show them to you over the teacups you would not be surprised or shocked. Would you? Not a bit of it. You would say: "That's a very pretty picture. Pray, what are they talking about, or of whom are they talking?"

Bodhidharma, Buddhist monks later introduced tea to Japan, claiming that it helped them stay alert while meditating. During tea's "golden age" in the eighth century, Lu Yü outlined that beverage's many aspects—from brewing to équipage to drinking—in the first book ever written about tea, *Ch'a Ching*, or The Classic of Tea. Originally designed to be read from panels of white silk, it is filled with learned advice. Regarding the manufacture of tea, he warns: "Do not pick on the day that has seen rain nor when clouds spoil the sky. Pick tea only on a clear day." He concludes that section with sage words about quality: "Its goodness is a decision for the mouth to make."

Lu Yü also suggested that "tea made from mountain streams is best, river water is all right, but well-water tea is quite inferior," adding that "if the evil genius of a stream makes the water bubble like a fresh spring, pour it out." (Today, many rely upon the virtues of water purifiers, which remove the taste of chlorine from tap water—the result is a brighter, more flavorful tea. Using bottled spring water of a reputable source is another option.) "The first cup," wrote Lu Yü, "should have a haunting flavor, strange and lasting."

Tea-drinking evolved to an art during the Sung Dynasty (A.D. 960-1279). In the sixteenth century, Japanese tea master, Sen Rikyû, ushered in a new era in the form of *chanoyu* (literally "hot water for tea"); the tradition continues today. During the Japanese tea ceremony, host and guests observe a heightened etiquette, each behaving with restraint and grace. The focus is on the *meaning* of the ceremony, rather than the actual tea itself.

Seafaring Dutch traders introduced tea to Europe. The Russians first learned of it in 1618, when a Mongol prince presented a gift of tea chests to Czar Romanov. By 1689, caravans of tea were traveling by camel the 11,000 miles between China and Russia known as the Silk Road. Samovars, those mysterious-looking urns, were used to brew and serve a strong, hearty tea to which jam was added—and often still is.

Britain's love affair with "tay" began in 1658. In a broadsheet entitled "An Exact Description of the Growth,

Quality and Virtues of the Leaf Tea," Thomas Garway, the first English tea dealer, noted, "In respect of its scarceness and dearness, it hath been only used as a regalia in high treatments and entertainments, and presents made thereof to princes and grandees."

King Charles II sipped green tea for both relaxation and pleasure, thus giving it credence; prior to that, it had been billed as a medicine and regarded with suspicion. Still, tea was slow to catch on because few families could afford it. In the 1700s, for example, a pound of tea cost one-third the average workman's weekly wage. It wasn't long before American colonists "hosted" the Boston Tea Party as a rebellion against tea taxes. Our independence today was born of those floating tea leaves in the harbor.

We have the Duchess of Bedford to applaud for Britain's afternoon tea custom. Back in the summer of 1840, she was loathe to pass the hour of five o'clock alone, so she invited a few friends to her Belvoir Castle boudoir, where she served them tea and cakes. Subsequent gatherings held in London (at which her guests were asked for "tea and a walking in the fields"), proved so popular, that other hostesses of the day promptly followed suit.

Tea's fate was brought full circle when it was found growing wild in India. "A discovery has been made of no less importance than that the hand of Nature has planted the shrub within the bounds of the wide dominion of Great Britain," declared G. G. Sigmond to the Royal Medico-Botanical Society. Many present-day inhabitants of India drink chai (boiled tea with milk, spices, and sugar), and that country has earned a reputation as a top tea producer, with thriving plantations in Assam and Darjeeling.

Kakuzo Okakura was born into a samurai family in Japan and later lived among artists in the States. In 1906 he wrote the classic *The Book of Tea*, in which he looks deep into "the cup of humanity": "The afternoon tea is now an important function in Western society. In the delicate clatter of trays and saucers, in the soft rustle of feminine hospitality, in the common catechism about cream and sugar, we know that the Worship of Tea is established beyond question." Tea is cast in

*K*ing Charles' Portuguese wife, Catherine of Barganza, brought to their marriage a dowry of many exotic teas, which, in turn, were shared with the court aristocracy. In a poem entitled "Of Tea Commended by Her Majesty," one grateful poet wrote: *The Muse's friend, Tea does our fancy aid,/Repress those vapours which the head invade,/And keep that palace of the soul serene.*

*T*hough the expense is considerable, the humblest peasant has his tea just like the rich man, observed La Rochefoucauld. Erik Geijer, a visitor to England, added, *Next to water tea is the Englishman's proper element. All classes consume it, and if one is out on the London streets early in the morning, one may see in many places small tables set up under the open sky, round which coal-carters and workmen empty their cups of the delicious beverage.*

an especially flattering light when he compares it to lesser beverages. "It has not the arrogance of wine, the self-consciousness of coffee, nor the simpering innocence of cocoa."

In 1946 George Orwell voiced his own opinions in an essay, "A Nice Cup of Tea," which was published in the *Evening Standard*. After concluding his eleven golden rules — among them, "One should take the teapot to the kettle and not the other way about" — he says, "There is also the mysterious social etiquette surrounding the teapot (why is it considered vulgar to drink out of your saucer, for instance?) and much might be written about the subsidiary uses of tea leaves, such as telling fortunes, predicting the arrival of visitors, feeding rabbits, healing burns, and sweeping the carpet."

Today tea follows common drinking water as the world's most popular beverage. It has earned a reputation for offering a range of health benefits as well, due to its high levels of antioxidant polyphenols known as catechins. In layman's terms, this means that tea — especially green tea — aside from stimulating our senses and teaching us about the "art of life" (as Okakura puts it), also has the potential to reduce chronic disease. *The New York Times* has reported that the substances found in tea "may lower blood pressure and blood cholesterol levels, stabilize blood sugar, kill decay-causing bacteria, block the action of many carcinogens and inhibit the growth of cancerous tumors." Similar sentiments were expressed centuries earlier, by Lu Yü: "If one is generally moderate but is feeling hot or warm, given to melancholia, suffering from aching of the brain, smarting of the eyes, troubled in the four limbs or afflicted in the hundred joints, he may take tea four or five times. Its liquor is like the sweetest dew of Heaven."

Though tea has had its share of disbelievers and naysayers, in 1641, the Dutch doctor, Nicholas Dirx, proclaimed that "nothing is comparable to this plant. Those who use it are for that reason alone exempt from all maladies and reach an extreme old age." (Dr. Dirx himself drank tea daily and enjoyed a long life.)

Throughout the ages, tea has been plucked (hence the mantra, "two leaves and a bud"), withered, rolled, fermented, fired, and, above all, cherished by those who have been fortunate enough to make its acquaintance. Its history is summed up well by Isaac D'Israeli. "The progress of this famous plant has been something like the progress of truth; suspected at first, though very palatable to those who had the courage to taste it; resisted as it encroached; abused as its popularity spread; and establishing its triumph at last, in cheering the whole land from the palace to the cottage, only by the slow and restless efforts of time and its own virtues." Tea has many forms. Black, green, oolong, white... To some, it is nothing less than nectar. If allowed to, it quenches the soul.

THE WAY OF TEA

By nature, tea is a deep and complicated subject. Roy Fong, owner of the Imperial Tea Court and a noted international expert in his field, had this to say when I asked him for his "tea philosophy": "I am not a philosopher, but I love the way of tea. One can safely say that no one will be able to learn of the knowledge of tea that has been accumulated for thousands of years, in a lifetime. I find that, after twenty years of devotion to this act, I am now only just scratching the surface. Tea continues to amaze me to no end."

The word "tea" originated from either of two Chinese words: *t'e* or *ch'a*, resulting in the following permutations: *Te, Tee, Tey, Teja, Thay, Thee, Thé, Tea, Thea...Cha, Ja, Tsa, Shai, Chay, Chai,* and *Tsai...* It would seem, then, that tea is a most appropriate drink for the new millennium, given its historical longevity and global appeal.

Whether a tea is picked by virgins, then cut with golden scissors (as in the Silver Needles lore), or monkey-picked (like Ti Kuan Yin once was), it retains a certain mystery. Don't forget that Sri Lanka was once called Ceylon and, before that, Serendip—while preparing this urban guide, I have heeded the fact that "serendipity" is defined as "an aptitude for making desirable discoveries by accident." In Tibet, tea (which is steeped for about an hour, mixed with salt, and churned with yak butter) is considered sacred. It is said that Shen Nung was born of a princess possessed by a dragon.

Thy amber-tinted drops bring back to me
Fantastic shapes of great Mongolian towers,
Emblazoned banners, and the booming gong;
I hear the sound of feast and revelry,
And smell, far sweeter than the sweetest flowers,
The kiosks of Peking, fragrant of Oolong!

Francis Saltus Saltus
"Tea," circa 1900

Yet even before the time of Shen Nung, archaeological evidence suggests that our prehistoric cousins, *Homo erectus pekinensis*, consumed tea's two main ingredients: tea leaves (from wild forest plants) and boiling water. "Better to be deprived of food for three days than of tea for one," goes the ancient Chinese saying. Some require the "froth of the liquid jade" for spiritual sustenance as well. Kakuzo Okakura (who coined the word *Teaism*), described the tearoom, or *sukiya*, as "an oasis in the dreary waste of existence where weary travelers could meet to drink from the common spring of art appreciation." The ceremony of tea, however crude it once was, adapts and evolves—San Francisco tea culture being no exception.

Especially if you have never before done so, consider attending a Japanese tea ceremony, which is based upon the simple acts of giving and receiving. Such an experience can be surprisingly profound. One thing is certain: though the form remains the same, no two ceremonies will ever be alike.

HOW TO USE THIS BOOK

This guide is divided into six categories:

Traditional—a very proper, British-style afternoon tea served in a first-class hotel or department store.

Cozy—a casual, British-style afternoon tea served in a small, often family-run tearoom. An intimate setting for tête-à-têtes.

Old World—tea with a Far Eastern flavor. Representing the traditional tearooms of China, Japan, and Taiwan, these establishments offer a range of experiences and exotic brews.

New World—featuring a new breed of tearoom, where one is poured a gourmet cup of tea and educated about the beauty and versatility of the leaf.

Offbeat—an eclectic blend of styles and fancies. Tea at the museum. Tea in a horticultural paradise.

Sip of Tea—an informal tea, featuring treats such as homemade crumpets, pastries, and chocolates. No-frills counter service.

Reservations are recommended for the Traditional category establishments (excluding Neiman Marcus), and for the Cozy tearooms (excluding The English Rose, King George Hotel, Tal-y-Tara, and The Village Green), though parties of four or more should always give some warning. At Tal-y-Tara, those wishing to order their specialty, Motorloaf, may want to call ahead. At Green Gulch Farm Zen Center, the Urasenke Foundation, and the Elizabeth F. Gamble Garden Center, not only are reservations required, but it is also requested that payment be made in advance. To avoid disappointment, you would be wise to book a table at Offbeat establishments Chai and O Chamé.

"Check, please."
The symbol of a teapot represents tea-time prices. (Tax and tip are not included.)

 Expect to pay around $15.00 to $20.00 and up (per person) for these classic afternoon teas. "Royal" teas, served with wine or champagne, cost more.

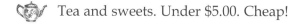 For a lovely afternoon tea, Japanese tea ceremony, or gourmet indulgence, from about $10.00 to $15.00.

$5.00 to $10.00 — set teas and à la carte.

Tea and sweets. Under $5.00. Cheap!

Understanding Tea
Loose-leaf teas are best; whenever a tea bag is offered instead of loose-leaf tea (as at the Sip of Tea places), I have made a note of it. Decaffeinated teas are also taken into account — though most herbal teas (also called infusions or, in French, *tisanes*), are, with the exception of maté and gotu kola, for example, naturally caffeine-free. (Actually, herbal teas are

The birth of the tea bag dates back to 1908, when American tea merchant Thomas Sullivan presented his customers with hand-sewn, silk sachets filled with samples of his tea. A few years earlier, a heat wave at the St. Louis World's Fair inspired Richard Blechynden, an Englishman, to invent the concoction known as iced tea.

not technically classified as teas, since they are not derived from the *Camellia sinensis* plant. On the other hand, flavored and scented teas are made with green, black, or oolong teas, to which flower blossoms or petals, spices, herbs, or the essential oils of fruits have been added.) There is a lesser-known tea (to those of us in the West) which deserves mention: *Matcha* is green, powdered tea, whisked with hot water to a mystical froth and served at Japanese tea ceremonies. People seem either to instantly love or despise it—as photographer Horace Bristol observed in a lovely essay about his experience at the Urasenke teahouse in Kyoto, it has "the consistency and color of a thin pea soup." Keep in mind, as you make your journey, that there are thousands of varieties of tea—from Assam to Lapsang Souchong. Like wine, each has a different appearance and flavor (described in tea-taster's terms as "bold" or "brassy" or "bright") and, as easily as it enchants one, it also evokes the faraway spirits of India, Africa, and the Far East.

What's in a Name?

Barron's Cooking Guide, *The New Food Lover's Companion*, by Sharon Tyler Herbst, states that "tarts can be bite-sized (often served as hors d'ouvres), individual-sized (sometimes called tartlets), or full-sized." I have used the words tart and tartlet interchangeably, in keeping with the idiosyncrasies of each tearoom's menu.

About clotted cream: In Britain, to attain this effect, the milk is left in a cool place for twenty-four hours, scalded, left out again, then the cream is skimmed from the top and refrigerated, having become suitably "clotted." Several hotels and tearooms mentioned in these pages serve clotted cream imported from Devon (calling it either "Devonshire," or "double Devon"). A few inspired chefs have concocted their own "mock" clotted cream variations, which taste nothing like the real thing, but have the distinct advantage of being fresh.

Special Teas

Vegetarians, please note that finger sandwich substitutions are available; you need only ask. The Ritz-Carlton has recently added a special Vegetarian Tea.

During the holidays, a few of the hotels (Fairmont, Park Hyatt, Ritz) and Chai host children's teas, which provide an introduction to the afternoon tea pastime for the younger set. (A pity one little boy I know missed this chance prior to his own bone-china-and-silver initation—a very expensive tantrum might have been avoided.) For a gingerbread-cookie-decorating experience (during which the adults have tea), see the listing for the Renaissance Stanford Court. These seasonal teas are quite popular; be sure to call well in advance to inquire about dates and times and to make a reservation.

For child-friendly tearooms with menus aimed at "wee ones," try The Butler's Pantry, Chai, Lisa's Tea Treasures, and Lovejoy's. The Japanese Tea Garden, with its Moon Bridge to climb and winding paths to wander, is also a great place for children. Consider too, attending the Pint-Sized Tea at The Ritz, and the Palace Hotel's regal Princess & Prince Tea.

What to Wear

Attire is left to the imagination. Dramatic hats are sometimes donned by women when attending a formal afternoon tea; men, though they are not required to wear jackets and ties, may  wish to. Tennis shoes and other athletic apparel (heaven forbid!) are frowned upon at the hotels. For a Japanese-style tea gathering, simple, comfortable clothing is suggested.

A WORD (OR TWO) ABOUT TRANSPORT

* For reasons of convenience and adventure (and for the environment's sake), I have tended to recommend public transportation. The Official San Francisco Street & Transit Map (available at bookstores) has helped me orient myself after my many dizzy rounds of tea and petits fours. For a bird's-eye view of tearoom locations at-a-glance, see maps and legend on pages 214-216.

* A cable car ride is an exciting way to travel to Nob Hill, though, if you wish to drive, see Useful Phone Numbers (page 211) for nearby parking garages. Valet parking is also a possibility at the hotels.

* Regarding cable cars: All of them—the PH, PM, and C—stop on Nob Hill, though only the PH and PM travel between downtown and Fisherman's Wharf. The PH (Powell-Hyde) runs between Powell & Market and Hyde & Beach. The PM (Powell-Mason) runs between Powell & Market and Taylor & Bay. The California (C) runs between California & Market and California & Van Ness.

* I encourage you to ride the F streetcar. These historic trolleys form a time-traveling fleet along Market Street.

* The CalTrain Station (connecting to Peninsula stations) is located at Fourth and Townsend Streets, south of Market. Sit on the upper level (east side) for a view of the surrealistic industrial wastelands, the junkyard statues, and the often sad-faced gamblers who have tested their luck at Bay Meadows race track. (Tip: The N-Judah streetcar stops at the CalTrain Station.)

* The Larkspur ferry departs from behind the Golden Gate Ferry Building (on the Embarcadero), at Pier "O."

* Also, please note that disabled access varies from place to place—the Japanese Tea Garden has a ramp, for instance, though the passage leading into the teahouse is narrow. Lady Pierrepont's has no ramp, but other arrangements can be made. The Elizabeth F. Gamble Garden Center has an elevator lift to the Main House. The teahouse at Green Gulch Farm Zen Center is reachable by a few steps (as are Lovejoy's and the loft at I Love Chocolate); the Urasenke Foundation tearoom is built upon a raised platform. (To participate in the Japanese tea ceremony, one traditionally sits or kneels on a straw mat; a pillow can be provided.) For A'Cuppa, enter through the Telesis Tower Lobby (Level 2) on Kearny Street. Though Chez Panisse's dining area is wheelchair accessible, the upstairs bar and café are not. Lisa's Tea Treasures in Menlo Park has, not one, but *two* ramps.

HAPPY SIPPING!

While I have tried to give as complete an overview as possible, please be aware that menus and prices will inevitably change; my apologies for any mistakes. Toward the end, you'll find **Tea Lovers' Resources**, listing associations, books, magazines and newsletters, a protocol school, tea ceremony classes, workshops, and celebrations, tea shops, mail-order tea, tea-time edibles (should you wish to host a tea party), teaware, and "virtual tea" (interesting and unusual web sites). Useful phone numbers for transport and parking garages are also included. You are invited to record your favorite tea experiences on the last pages, in Tea Notes.

Sip by sip, friends and families reunite over teacups. Conversations, about everything from affairs of the heart to metaphysics, flourish. As one spreads lemon curd upon one's scone, the world itself often seems less harsh, its problems dreamily smoothed out. Enchantment reigns. Whether it be tearoom or tea garden, each of the establishments listed herein provides a suitable place at which to recover from the rigorous demands of modern living. Of course, something must also be said for the humble cup of tea, taken at home, in the fleeting space of solitude.

"Tea is drunk to forget the din of the world," observed the sage, T'ien Yiheng, in his 16th-century diary. The art of tea, if fully explored, has much to teach us. Slow down...savor the delicious moment. Enjoy!

Yours in tea,

Ulrica Hume

p.s. If you know of a worthy tearoom not mentioned in these pages, please send your suggestion to:

Blue Circle Press
P.O. Box 460055
San Francisco, CA 94146

tea-mail: uhume@compuserve.com

TRADITIONAL

The Fairmont's Lobby Lounge, circa 1950

FAIRMONT HOTEL
LOBBY LOUNGE

I always like to make a pilgrimage to The Fairmont during the holidays, when the lobby is decked out with a large tree. One year, the flocked boughs were trimmed with Alice-in-Wonderland ornaments; another time, Santa in his sleigh floated miraculously overhead.

On this occasion, however, the lobby had resumed its usual state of elegance, and a dignified elderly couple, guided by their small dog and a wayward cane, were slowly making their way along the fantastic red and black swirls of carpet.

According to Mr. Wolfe, the Concierge Director, most people, when seeing the lobby for the first time, "act like it's the Vatican." Renowned decorator Dorothy Draper envisioned a grand Venetian palace when she was called upon to transform the lobby in the late 1940s. Roman busts and columns combine with a bold color scheme to reflect the rakish charm, romance, and flamboyance of San Francisco's Golden Age.

Back in 1902, the Fair sisters (Tessie and Virginia) set out to build The Fairmont Hotel as a monument to their late father, "Bonanza Jim," who had made his fortune from a Nevada silver mine. However, by 1906, they felt burdened by this task, and, before the hotel opened, they sold it to Herbert and Hartland Law, two enterprising brothers. Days later, the 1906 earthquake struck and although the building survived the jolts, it was destroyed by fire. Gertrude Atherton, a writer, was crossing the Bay at the time: "I forgot the doomed city as I gazed at The Fairmont, a tremendous volume of white smoke pouring from the roof, every window a shimmering sheet of gold; not a flame, nor a spark shot forth. The Fairmont will never be as demonic in its beauty again."

Today, in the lobby's mazelike corridors, photographs with titles like "Ruins of Chinatown" and "The Burning City" document the disaster. Hard to believe that San Francisco was once so devastated — looking at these images before tea, I was reminded of the ruins of Pompeii.

Promptly at three o'clock, harpist Vicki Demartini-Ruggeri, dressed in a black velvet gown, a cameo pinned to her white embroidered collar, began plucking the strings of her Wurlitzer. Soon I found myself daydreaming as I sipped bergamot-flavored **Earl Grey** from a dainty cup of Royal Doulton china. (Other HARNEY & SONS teas include **Black Currant, Ceylon and India, Darjeeling, Egyptian Chamomile, English Breakfast, Hot Cinnamon Spice**, and **Jasmine**.) Almost against my will, I felt the aristocratic upward pull of my pinkie finger. Now everything seemed to be in order.

The two-tiered tray presented a cornucopia of English Afternoon Tea delights: pastries (among them a kiwi tartlet and a chocolate petit four); a currant scone dusted with powdered sugar, accompanied by preserves and clear glass cups of Devonshire clotted cream and homemade lemon curd; and five unadorned finger sandwiches (cucumber with watercress, salmon with cream cheese and dill, chicken salad, sliced ham, and egg salad).

There was a rustle of sheet music. I was enjoying the hypnotic, ticktock melody of Pachelbel's Canon in D, when a family of four was seated across from me on a low red settee draped with fringe: mother, father, child, and grandmother. How would the boy, who looked to be about four years old, cope with the ritual of afternoon tea? Would the demands of etiquette prove too great?

Just as I had feared, the child soon became unruly. He squirmed and moaned as the harpist stoically continued, his sobs and screeches echoing in the vast lobby. He was pulled away from the table by his father — for some "time out" — and then brought back, after some agitated whispering.

I was thinking of The Fairmont's annual Gingerbread Theatre Tea — how Santa and his kindly elves serve the children hot chocolate, finger sandwiches, pastries, and cookies inside a life-sized gingerbread house — when the harpist launched into "Somewhere Over the Rainbow." The child wiped his tears and forced down a gulp of tea. He tasted his scone. Then, with amazement, he watched as a red-coated porter (who resembled one of the Wicked Witch's cursed monkeys), rushed past.

What would he remember of this day, I wondered later.

In his wake, he had left behind only a few crumbs, a rumpled napkin, and a teacup half full of amber-colored liquid.

FAIRMONT HOTEL
950 Mason Street (at California), on Nob Hill
San Francisco, CA 94108

Phone	(415) 772-5000, hotel; (415) 772-5281, afternoon tea reservations. *Please note: Renovation of the Lobby Lounge is scheduled to begin in 1999. Tea service will be temporarily suspended.*
Web	http://www.fairmont.com
Hours	Friday and Saturday, 3:00 p.m.–6:00 p.m. Sunday, 1:00 p.m.–6:00 p.m.
Transport	* California cable car to California and Mason * Powell cable car to Powell and California Walk up California Street one block to Mason.
Price	🫖 🫖 🫖 🫖
Established	Original hotel (the first on Nob Hill), 1906. Afternoon tea has been served in the Lobby Lounge and the Cirque Room since the hotel re-opened in 1907.

ENGLISH AFTERNOON TEA
A LA CARTE SELECTION
CHAMPAGNES, PORTS, AND SHERRIES
GINGERBREAD THEATRE TEA (CHRISTMAS)

Stands the church clock at ten to three?
And is there honey still for tea?

Rupert Brooke (1887–1915)
The Old Vicarage, Grantchester

MARK HOPKINS HOTEL
TOP OF THE MARK

Though the newly remodeled Top of the Mark, with its dance floor and spectacular 360-degree city view, has been primarily known as a cocktail lounge/nightclub, now it is also a place where, for a price, tea-drinkers can feel at home. Ride the special elevator to the rarefied world of the nineteenth floor. (That is, unless you suffer from acrophobia, the dread of high places.) The decor—a wall of mirrors, bold striped chairs, and touches of wrought iron—by Beverly Hills designer Tim Zebrowski, is refined and a bit eclectic, befitting a true San Francisco tea experience. Be sure to see *Window Washer*, an amazing photograph by Ansel Adams, which was taken in 1939 when the Top of the Mark first opened. It is on display in the room's northeast corner.

I inadvertently picked the anniversary of the 1906 earthquake to visit the Top of the Mark. As the elevator rose, I recalled how not only The Fairmont Hotel, but the Stanford and Hopkins mansions were also lost to fire. It is no small feat that today these three Nob Hill hotels stand in place of ashes and dashed dreams.

My waiter, Richard Varga, a debonair fellow sporting a bronze-and-beige uniform, presented me with a large wooden tea chest, in which THE TEA COMPANY teas, like fine cigars, awaited my selection. What would it be? **Darjeeling**? A tisane of organic chamomile, lavender, and lemon peel called **Trilogy**? Finally, the dark and earthy-looking **Russian Caravan** tea took my fancy. (Other teas include **Earl Grey, Emerald Rice, Jasmine Pearls, Lemon Mint,** and **Mark Hopkins Blend**).

I leaned back. I was admiring the view when it began to rain. As water streamed down the windows, I thought of the Top of the Mark's so-called Weeping Corner, where, during World War II, flocks of wistful women watched as Pacific-bound ships carrying their husbands and sweethearts passed under the Golden Gate Bridge. The rain intensified, obscuring the spire of Grace Cathedral and the people far below, who, from this height, appeared no larger than sugar cubes.

Ricardo Scales took his place at the baby grand and set a spirited, romantic mood by playing, among other familiar tunes, "I Only Have Eyes for You." A couple drifted by in search of a private table. They ordered drinks, the woman leaning forward to take the man's hand once Richard the waiter had turned on his heels to alert the barman of their order. They were not overly aware of the view. Liaison? I wondered. Everything seemed to be going well until the man's cellular phone rang. The woman frowned, looked miffed—*not now! not here!*—as he took the call.

I was diverted from my people-watching by the arrival of the peculiar, white Ronnefeldt teapot. Resembling an object from one of Picasso's abstract paintings, it rested on its side, spout pointing up like the raised trunk of an elephant. Next, an egg timer was placed on my table and flicked over, so that the sand began to fall. Apparently, my tea was to steep in the teapot's dam for exactly three minutes.

I felt in awe of this teapot, and worried that I might spill the brew when I righted it to its normal position and poured. Fortunately, this didn't happen, though I felt its daunting presence for the remainder of the afternoon. (Note: These teapots have since been replaced.)

The *prix fixe* tea tray towered before me. Scones, in varieties of currant and chocolate chip, were accompanied by double Devon clotted cream, jam, and honey. Four impressive "petite savory sandwiches"—prawn with jewels of red and gold caviar, trout with mango salsa, salmon with cream cheese and black caviar, and goat cheese with mushroom and sun-dried tomatoes—were as enjoyable to eat as they were to behold. I am pleased to report that the pastries—a fruit tartlet, strawberry mousse, and hazelnut chocolate cake—baked by pastry chef Lori Raji, can best be described in layman's terms as "yummy."

Towards the end of my tea, I happened to glance again at the couple; the man was still talking on his phone, oblivious to the woman, whose face matched the gloaming and the approaching storm-clouds outside.

MARK HOPKINS HOTEL
999 California Street (at Mason), on Nob Hill
San Francisco, CA 94108

Phone	(415) 392-3434, hotel; (415) 616-6916, afternoon tea reservations
Web	http://www.interconti.com
Hours	Monday–Friday, 3:00 p.m.–5:00 p.m. Piano entertainment, 4:00 p.m.–8:00 p.m. Closed Saturday and Sunday
Transport	* California cable car to California and Mason * Powell cable car to Powell and California Walk up California Street one block to Mason.
Price	
Established	Original mansion, 1878. Hotel, 1926. Afternoon tea has been served in the lobby on and off since the hotel opened, and at the Top of the Mark since 1996.

PRIX FIXE AFTERNOON TEA FOR ADULTS
PRIX FIXE AFTERNOON TEA FOR CHILDREN (HALF PRICE)

Love and scandal are the best sweeteners of tea.

Henry Fielding (1707–1754)
Love in Several Masques

NEIMAN MARCUS
THE ROTUNDA

The phrase "shop 'til you drop" takes on new meaning at Neiman Marcus. Say you've just spent six-hundred-and-seventy-six dollars on a turtle-shaped tureen. My advice? Head for the Rotunda on the fourth floor. Find a cozy booth, or sit by the large windows overlooking Union Square. A lovely stained glass dome (which graced the City of Paris department store when it occupied this same site) depicts a ship tossed on waves. The Latin inscription translates, "It floats, but does not sink." On either side of the historic dome are depicted two scowling Winds.

The Rotunda doubles as a restaurant and tearoom. The tea list comprises **British Breakfast, Chamomile, Chrysanthemum Mint, Darjeeling, Earl Grey, Jasmine Pearls,** and **Neiman Marcus Blend**—all by THE TEA COMPANY. Recent converts to loose-leaf tea, the staff seemed genuinely inspired and were quick to show me, by snipping open a tea bag, the "dust" found in "an inferior Darjeeling."

Teapots (fitted with internal strainers) hail from Chatsford, England. The teacups themselves are short and squat. Bottled like spices, the teas may be purchased in the adjacent Epicure shop, which is reminiscent of the Food Halls of Harrods. There you'll encounter everything from chocolate to caviar—and even a few industrial-looking teapots.

I selected the Afternoon Tea, though the Petite Cream Tea was a tempting alternative. A two-tiered, doilied tray arrived, bearing finger sandwiches (chicken salad, prosciutto ham with walnut and blue cheese spread, watercress with butter, smoked salmon, and cucumber with cream cheese), sweet cream and preserves, and a variety of subtle-tasting pastries. The combination of chocolate scone with Jasmine Pearls tea was quite decadent indeed. The Neiman Marcus Blend, which I also sampled, was strong and distinctive—a good shopper's tonic.

Stars such as Kevin Costner, Don Johnson, and Holly Hunter have visited The Rotunda, as have many local television news personalities, though I cannot verify whether they indulged in afternoon tea.

Wandering in the store later, I made the acquaintance of Greg Kramer of Children's World. Learning of my interest in tea, he promptly led me to Intimate Apparel, where, among the silken shrouds of lingerie, we encountered a tea service (circa 1930). He explained that it had been rescued from a sunken Italian cruise ship. There was something undeniably charming about this tea service, despite its dents and nicks. The silver-plated nickel shone with a rosy cast, and the bone handles possessed a quaint, if homely, appeal. "How much?" I asked, forgetting for a moment that this was a store that specialized in Chanel, Luis Vuitton, Armani. He paused. "That would be...eighteen-hundred dollars."

Needless to say, I didn't buy it. Closer to my price range would have been the "recycled" British hotel ware—the toast rack from The Ritz, the creamer from Claridges, and the unmatched silver—all with stories to tell, I'm sure.

NEIMAN MARCUS
150 Stockton Street (at Geary)
San Francisco, CA 94108

Phone	(415) 362-3900, Neiman Marcus; (415) 362-4777, The Rotunda
Web	http://www.neimanmarcus.com
Hours	Every day, 2:30 p.m.–5:00 p.m.
Transport	From Powell and Market, walk up Powell Street three blocks to Union Square. Turn right on Geary and walk one block to Stockton Street.
Price	
Established	1982

AFTERNOON TEA
PETITE CREAM TEA
PORTS AND SHERRIES

PALACE HOTEL
THE GARDEN COURT

Take tea among palms and philodendrons in a downtown conservatory setting. Horse-drawn carriages once delivered the guests of this landmark luxury hotel, which was the first of its kind west of the Mississippi. In 1945, The Garden Court hosted the official banquet for the opening of the United Nations. Presidents, kings, queens, and other men and women of influence—from Rockefeller, Carnegie, and Vanderbilt, to D. H. Lawrence and Amelia Earhart—have stayed at the hotel. So have Madam Chiang Kai-shek, Thomas Edison, and Enrico Caruso (who fled not long after the 1906 earthquake).

Today, The Garden Court is a gold-leafed vision of opulence, with twinkling Austrian crystal chandeliers and giant marble columns. This is an ideal tea spot for bridal showers and other festive celebrations. Afternoon light filters in through the dome's white stained glass far above, creating an airy, cathedral-like atmosphere, while Katherine Honey teases the strings of her harp, playing "As Time Goes By."

Shying from the Palace Champagne Tea and the Sparkling Wine Tea, I chose instead the Garden Court Tea with a pot of **Palace Blend**. A spirited tea, the Palace Blend is scented with mango, peach, orange peel, cinnamon sticks, and cloves. The tea selection features only THE REPUBLIC OF TEA teas: **All Day Breakfast, Blackberry Sage, Darjeeling, Dragon Well, Earl Greyer, Ginger Peach, Jasmine Jazz, Mango Ceylon** (regular and decaf) **Moroccan Mint, Tea of Inquiry,** and **Ti Kuan Yin**; few traditional black teas are offered. The herbal teas are **Chamomile Lemon, Ginseng Peppermint, Kid's Cuppa, Lemon Wintergreen,** and **Organic Temple of Health**.

My scone I slathered in rose petal jam (imported from Greece), homemade lemon curd, and rich, fluffy crème fraîche (not clotted cream). Four finger sandwiches awaited: the first a delicate white rectangle of cucumber slices arranged on a spread of cream cheese and watercress, garnished with Feta sprinkles, which I quickly devoured. On to the brown bread striped with green zucchini and yellow squash strips, this time

The Palace's Garden Court, then...

...and now

on a black olive spread. (Both sandwiches were garnished with a sun-dried-tomato-and-cream-cheese rosette, which I irrationally mistook for Cheez Whiz.) Next, a brown bread triangle of smoked salmon and black caviar (lime-green *wasabi* caviar is sometimes served), and, on a circle of white bread, prosciutto rolled with pâté, topped by a melon ball.

Fruit tarts — kiwi with blackberry and pecan — though not homemade, provided a welcome contrast to the sandwiches. These fruit types change, however, so don't be alarmed to find a grape tart decorated with shaves of chocolate. And finally, pastries: a chocolate-dipped strawberry, shortbread, mocha tart, and a chocolate-pistachio petit four.

I was perplexed when the dreamy and serene little girl at the next table received a jeweled, silver tiara and a colorful lollipop scepter — that is, until the harpist began playing "Happy Birthday." Apparently, the child, who was accompanied by her mother, had ordered the Princess & Prince Tea. (Please note that reservations are required for this tea.) As a way of catering to the fussiness of children, egg salad, peanut butter, and jelly finger sandwiches (the latter with candied sprinkles) are served with assorted tea pastries. Most children will be amused by the maraschino cherry balanced upon a squiggle of peanut butter. Parties of up to twenty children have descended upon the spacious Garden Court at one time. "They behaved extremely well," General Manager Robert Faure tactfully informed me.

After my tea, I strolled along the Main Promenade, past tapestries and dark, somber paintings, stopping to study the fascinating displays of old photos, books, and Palace Hotel memorabilia such as matchbooks, menus, a guest room key from 1920, silver egg holders, and Bavarian china spittoons. Also of interest were a beaded silk bodice (circa 1890), a black feather fan and parasol, a derby hat, wire-rimmed eyeglasses, and a gramophone.

In Maxfield's Bar, an original Maxfield Parrish, "The Pied Piper," rivals the two TVs on either side of it, which broadcast sports. Upstairs, in the balcony French Parlor, which overlooks The Garden Court, members of the Ladies Auxiliary once sat and gossiped — and perhaps still do.

PALACE HOTEL
2 New Montgomery Street (at Market)
San Francisco, CA 94105

Phone	(415) 512-1111, hotel; (415) 546-5089, afternoon tea reservations
Web	http://www.sheraton.com
Hours	Wednesday–Saturday, 2:00 p.m.–4:30 p.m. Closed Sunday, Monday, Tuesday
Transport	Muni bus, Metro, F streetcar (historic trolley), or BART to Montgomery Station. (If arriving underground, take the New Montgomery exit.) New Montgomery Street is on the south side of Market, between Second and Third Streets.
Price	
Established	Original hotel, 1875; rebuilt in 1909 after fires resulting from the earthquake. The Garden Court, formerly a carriage entrance, has been serving afternoon tea ever since.

PALACE CHAMPAGNE TEA
SPARKLING WINE TEA
GARDEN COURT TEA
PRINCESS & PRINCE TEA (INCLUDES CROWN AND SCEPTER)

*I believe it is customary in good society
to take some light refreshment at five o'clock.*

Oscar Wilde
The Importance of Being Earnest, 1895

Park Hyatt Hotel
The Library

The Park Hyatt is an accordion-shaped skyscraper, located near the heart of the Financial District and the Embarcadero Center. And yet this modern exterior belies what is concealed inside. Pass through the revolving doors, and that glass-and-concrete jungle is swiftly exchanged for a lobby of neoclassical formality and refinement.

The ambience is like that of a private club. Australian lace-wood and polished Italian granite delight the eye, while exotic, hand-woven carpets endure the tread of the hotel's many European guests. In the bar lounge, cigars such as the pricey Anniversario #2, Robustos, and Rothschilds are sold.

Touring the lobby, I discovered *Alquimia LXXIV*, an attractive, gold-leaf linen weaving, and other commissioned works of art (many more of which are shown throughout the first three floors of the hotel — ask the concierge for the "Art in the Park" self-guided tour brochure). In the center of the spiral staircase, Arnaldo Pomodoro's enormous bronze sculpture *Colonna* stands like the trunk of a magical tree. Near the elevators, *Woolly Mammoth*, a small beast balanced atop a pillar, seems a bit out of place, however.

The non-smoking Library, which occupies a quiet corner of the lobby, is distinguished by its wall of books, a grandfather clock, two chessboard tables, and a world globe. Here, among the fan palms and peace lilies, the lords and ladies of the business world often gather.

I took tea at a chessboard table, where books such as *The Woman He Loved* by Ralph G. Martin, *The Measure of the Hours* by Maeterlinck, and *Cabbages and Kings* by O. Henry were within reach. I had just spotted the volumes of the 1929 Encyclopedia Britannica, when my waiter, David Goodness, approached.

Service is paramount at the Park Hyatt. The white embroidered placemat seemed to float down upon my table. Next came the Wedgwood bone china. A bowl of brown and white sugar cubes and a pair of tongs were deftly arranged. I spoke the words "English Hotel Tea, please," and he was off, like a gazelle, to fetch my pot of **Verveine** tea (imported from France).

Other "international" teas by HARNEY & SONS come from faraway places: **Darjeeling** (the Himalayas); **Ceylon and India** blend (Sri Lanka and India); **Chamomile** (Egypt); **English Breakfast, Jasmine,** and **Lapsang Souchong** (China). The **Earl Grey** originates from four different countries: China, India, Sri Lanka, and Formosa. **Black Currant** tea (China and Sri Lanka); **Hot Cinnamon Spice** (Sri Lanka, India, and Vietnam); and **Peppermint** (all the way from the Yakima valley of Oregon, U.S.A.), are also options.

My Verveine tea (made from the verbena plant, a holy bough once carried by priests) provided a good contrast to the exquisite fare, which is served in courses, rather than all at once. Warm, fresh-baked scones with whipped Devonshire clotted cream (which tasted like crème fraîche) and strawberry preserves were followed by tea sandwiches (cucumber and cream cheese, chopped egg with caviar, chicken salad, deviled ham, and salmon with cream cheese and capers), which were artfully constructed of light, fluffy sourdough or dark rye in the form of geometric shapes. And then the Christofle crystal cart rolled to a stop before me. Pastries, by chef Robert Cheong, tempted. Finally, after much consideration, I chose an adorable miniature eclair, a lemon bar, and a chocolate confection topped by a sugared violet.

"Is everything to your liking?" Mr. Goodness asked, as piano music — "Ain't Misbehavin'" — laughter, and the gentle clinking of silverware drifted in from the nearby bar lounge. I dabbed my mouth, glanced down at the bare Wedgwood. "Oh, yes!" I replied. How could it be otherwise?

Large tea parties can be accommodated upstairs, in the restaurant on the third floor. At Christmastime, there is a Teddy Bear Tea for children. Served on china, it includes hot chocolate or cider, peanut butter and jelly or bologna and cheese finger sandwiches, gingerbread or chocolate chip cookies, and M&M brownies. Each child also receives a teddy bear gift.

Teddy Bear Tea at the Park Hyatt

PARK HYATT HOTEL
333 Battery Street (at Clay)
San Francisco, CA 94111

Phone   (415) 392-1234

Web   http://www.hyattsf.com

Hours   Every day, 3:00 p.m.–4:30 p.m.

Transport   * Muni bus or F streetcar (historic trolley) to
                  First and Market. Please note that First Street
                  becomes Battery on the north side of Market.
                  Walk up Battery four blocks to Clay Street.
                  * Metro or BART to either Montgomery or
                  Embarcadero Stations. Battery Street is
                  between these stations, on the north side of
                  Market. Walk up Battery four blocks to Clay
                  Street.

Price

Established   1989

TEA ROYALE
ENGLISH HOTEL TEA
AFTERNOON TEA BREAK
TEDDY BEAR TEA (CHRISTMAS)
A LA CARTE SELECTION
DAILY SELECTION OF CHEF ROBERT CHEONG'S PASTRIES

*There are few hours in life more agreeable than
the hour dedicated to the ceremony known as afternoon tea.*

Henry James (1843–1916)
Portrait of a Lady

Renaissance Stanford Court Hotel
Lobby Lounge

Follow the ivy-covered wall to the inner courtyard of the Renaissance Stanford Court Hotel, past the trickling Beaux-Arts fountain surrounded by urns of flowers. In the lobby, under a dome of Tiffany-style stained glass, a sepia-tone mural by Evans & Brown depicts San Francisco's lively history. Leland Stanford, founder of Stanford University and former California governor and U.S. senator, appears alongside African-Americans of the Victorian era; other panels show old Chinatown, native California Indians, and the 1849 Gold Rush.

The Stanford Mansion, first of its kind on Nob Hill, was destroyed by fire in the 1906 earthquake. But the Renaissance Stanford Court hotel, with its 19th-century facade, is relatively young; it opened in 1972, replacing the Stanford Court Apartments, which were built in 1912 by a real estate investor named Lucien H. Sly. Today, in the lobby, like portals to the past, black-and-white photographs give glimpses of "The Hill of Palaces" in its heyday.

The elegant but unpretentious Renaissance Stanford Court is a haven from the downtown swirl of deadlines and meetings. Here one can watch the distant cable cars lurching up and down California Street. The hotel is decorated in a unique and tasteful Italianate style, mirroring the mood of the mansion, and thereby conjuring the spirit of the place. A prominent painting in the tea lounge (which staff refer to as "The Opera Painting") spotlights a woman in a feather hat, a red-coated gentleman doing a jig, and a pensive greyhound in the foreground. Who are they? you might wonder, as you recline upon the long blue settee.

Treasures for viewing include an original Maxfield Parrish, *Old White Birch* (circa 1930s), a porcelain Imari vase, and a large clock, which was a gift from Napoleon Bonaparte to his Minister of War in 1806. Worth a peek is the mysterious, octagonal basket near the concierge's desk. Children will want to experience the strange audio effect by speaking underneath one of two Baccarat crystal chandeliers (which once lit the Paris

Palace Hotel).

I visited the Stanford Court on a breezy spring day and settled myself into a comfortable leather-upholstered chair near a small window filled with well-tended plants and a quirky view of the city.

Feeling famished, I ordered the Full Tea. My zesty tea — **Hot Cinnamon Spice** — was served in a small white teapot. Other HARNEY & SONS teas include **Ceylon and India, Darjeeling** (known as "The Champagne of Teas"), **Earl Grey, English Breakfast, Formosa Oolong, Jasmine,** and **Sencha** (a Japanese everyday tea). There is also a decaffeinated tea. The herbal offerings are **Egyptian Chamomile** and **Peppermint**.

The wobbly three-tiered tray had a distinct air of the 1970s. Though I was pleased with the miniature scones, the Devonshire clotted cream seemed to me a bit *too* clotted. Finger sandwiches — egg and chive on white bread, cucumber and tomato with cream cheese on brioche, chicken and watercress with mascarpone on whole wheat, and smoked salmon with crème fraîche and caviar on pumpernickel — rounded out the Full Tea. The Light Tea and The Stanford Court Tea are also options.

Working my way down the tiers I encountered tea cookies, fresh fruit tartlets, and a petit four. These bakery-made treats were all delicious. One tea cookie seemed to melt in my mouth. The lemon tartlet was decorated by a dainty dollop of meringue.

During the holidays, children are welcomed to decorate gingerbread cookies with — who else? — Santa Claus, while their parents take tea nearby. There is no extra charge for this memorable opportunity.

Tea won't be complete unless you stop by John Small Ltd., an authentic British gift shop located in the lobby which specializes in thematic (regimental, historical, and U.S. university) buttons and cufflinks. The tiny shop, watched over by proprietor John Small himself (and a portrait of Churchill), also stocks badges, jewelry, and coasters. "Suits, too?" I asked, amazed by the myriad goods. "Not suits, *blazers*!" he was quick to correct me.

RENAISSANCE STANFORD COURT HOTEL
905 California Street (at Powell), on Nob Hill
San Francisco, CA 94108

Phone	(415) 989-3500
Web	http://www.renaissancehotels.com
Hours	Every day, 2:30 p.m.–5:00 p.m.
Transport	* Powell cable car to Powell and California * California cable car to California and Powell
Price	
Established	Original mansion, 1876. Hotel, 1972. Afternoon tea has been served in the Lobby Lounge since the hotel opened.

THE STANFORD COURT TEA
FULL TEA
LIGHT TEA
A LA CARTE SELECTION
SHERRIES

Here thou, great Anna! whom three realms obey,
Dost sometimes counsel take—and sometimes tea.

Alexander Pope
The Rape of the Lock, 1714

RITZ-CARLTON HOTEL
LOBBY LOUNGE

This 1909 landmark building, with its great Ionic columns and imposing façade, was once the headquarters of the Metropolitan Life Insurance Company—in fact, their guardian angel can still be seen, perched high on the roof, reminding one to buy insurance. In 1987, The Ritz-Carlton began renovating the "temple of commerce's" interior, creating a hotel where offices had once stood. Designer Frank Nicholson was called upon to give it that Ritz touch. The result is a five-star wonderland, waiting behind a rather cold and pompous curtain of stone.

The Ritz-Carlton is the sister hotel to the famous Ritz in London, which is one of *the* best places to have tea across the pond. Knowing that the hotel's aim is "to fulfill even the unexpressed wishes of our guests," I happily scanned the menu and ordered the Full Tea with a pot of **English Breakfast**. Almost immediately, my Wedgwood teapot in a Kutani Crane motif appeared, along with a crystal tray of cream, tong, and sugars.

Everything was just so. The fairy-tale setting is much like the parlor of a turn-of-the-century mansion. The peach walls were trimmed in the color of clotted cream, and the drapes were lush. Cobalt-blue vases dotting the tables each held a single rose. Above the bar, a mirror endlessly reflected chandeliers, creating the sense of a tunnel leading back through time. But perhaps most impressive of all was the grey-and-white marble working fireplace and the clock on its mantle with the mischievous black cherub marking twelve.

The ritual of afternoon tea has a calming effect. As I sat beneath the *Portrait of Miss Nelson*, near a French silk tapestry of a dancing muse, I took the opportunity to eavesdrop on the other guests. At a nearby table, a large, distinguished-looking party discussed everything from opium to real estate. Glasses of champagne cocktails clinked. Many of the women wore hats—grand straw hats, in black and white, with wide ribbons or ropy braids, and provocative, upturned

Afternoon Tea at The Ritz-Carlton

brims.

To the tune of the harpist Paula Abrams-Wilson's "When You Wish Upon a Star," the waitress glided towards me, bearing the three-tiered tray. I began with the tiny apricot-blueberry tartlet, madeleine, and florentine on the top tier, then proceeded to the middle tier's open-faced finger sandwiches: Norwegian smoked salmon with pickled onion and caviar, prosciutto ham with asparagus tips, egg with chives. And my favorite: cucumber with Roquefort and walnuts. The currant scone, on the third tier, I layered with homemade lemon curd and whipped Devonshire clotted cream.

And still there were tea cakes!—banana and lemon poppy seed. And shortbread.

Teas are all by HARNEY & SONS: **Ceylon and India, China Rose Petal, Darjeeling, Earl Grey, Formosa Oolong, Gunpowder Green** (named for its rolled, pellet-shaped leaves, which the Chinese call *Zhucha*, or Pearl Tea), and **Lapsang Souchong**. Flavored (**Black Currant, Hot Cinnamon Spice, Jasmine, Peach and Passion Fruit, Spiced Orange**) and herbal teas (**Chamomile, Peppermint**) are also available.

A new addition to the menu is the Vegetarian Tea. Similar to the Full Tea, it features the following finger sandwiches, which might also appeal to carnivores: eggplant pesto on rye bread, vegetable terrine (similar to pâté) on dark rye, tomatoes and mozzarella on focaccia, and grilled vegetables on focaccia with tapenade (a spicy thick sauce which comes from the Provence region of France).

For special occasions, call in advance and request a message—such as "Welcome to San Francisco!" or "Happy Birthday!"—to be written in chocolate on the plate.

The Ritz hosts a Pint-Sized Tea for Two on Saturdays, a Make-Your-Own-Puppet tea and puppet show, and a Ghost and Goblin costume tea. During the holidays, there is a daily Teddy Bear Tea, at which each child receives his or her own teddy bear. (Children are invited to bring their own teddy bears along, if desired.) Peanut butter and jelly, ham and cheese, tuna, and egg salad finger sandwiches are served, along with cookies, gummy bears, and a fruit tartlet. Instead of tea, young guests sip hot chocolate with miniature marshmallows. The harpist reads two stories, a sing-a-long is conducted — and then out comes a giant teddy bear, who hugs and poses for keepsake photographs with the sticky-faced (though no doubt well-dressed) children.

RITZ-CARLTON HOTEL
600 Stockton Street (at California), on Nob Hill
San Francisco, CA 94108

Phone	(415) 296-7465, hotel; (415) 773-6198, afternoon tea reservations
Web	http://www.ritzcarlton.com
Hours	Monday–Friday, 2:30 p.m.–4:30 p.m. Saturday and Sunday, 1:00 p.m.–4:30 p.m.
Transport	* Powell cable car to Powell and California. Walk down California Street one block to Stockton Street. * California cable car to California and Stockton. (Please note that, on the north side of California Street, between Stockton and Powell, there is an enchanting statue, *Resting Hermes*.) * Or, from Union Square, head north on Stockton Street, taking the stairway when Stockton Street enters tunnel.
Price	
Established	Metropolitan Life, 1909. Hotel, 1991

ROYAL TEA
FULL TEA
VEGETARIAN TEA
LIGHT TEA
CAVIAR
DESSERTS
CHAMPAGNES, PORTS, AND SHERRIES,
SPARKLING WINES AND CHAMPAGNE COCKTAILS
TEDDY BEAR TEA (CHRISTMAS) *$2.00 DONATED TO THE MAKE-A-WISH FOUNDATION*

St. Francis Hotel
The Compass Rose

The Compass Rose, so named after t͟ found in the background of compasses, is a d̲ filled with artwork and artifacts from aro͟ᵤ ᵥorld. Originally named The Café when the hotel opened in 1904, in 1913 it was converted to a library, becoming the haunt of literati such as Mark Twain and Ernest Hemmingway. In 1939, to the horror of many, books were replaced by bottles of liquor. The Patent Leather Bar, as it was then called, evolved into The Terrace Room, and finally The Compass Rose, which, oddly enough, looks quite similar to the original Café.

One thing is certain: The Compass Rose has plenty of character. Screens, fluted wood columns, and large potted trees divide the large room into intimate nooks, where, among mosaic marble tables, cloisonné vases, and cobra lamps, you can blissfully disappear behind your teacup.

I sat by one of the tall, arched windows overlooking Union Square, watching windblown people passing by on cable cars. Occasionally I could hear the carnival-like toot-tooting of the doormen's Acme whistles. To my left I noticed, among many other treasures, a silk wedding robe emblazoned with the symbol of the phoenix. The phoenix is a beautiful mythical bird who dies by fire and is reborn out of ash—an odd choice for a wedding robe. Near the table where television executives were in the midst of making a deal hung a bizarre painting of two monkeys, in which one serenaded the other on a mandolin. Behind me, the portrait of a forlorn woman showed her decked out in a white tea gown, slouch hat, and golden shawl, standing alone in a pastoral setting. The tilt of her head suggested compassion, perhaps even weariness.

Racing from table to table, bearing teapots, the servers resembled magic genies in their brown silk belted tunics. I unfolded my mauve napkin as Paul Lehman, who hails from Hamburg, set before me the imposing three-tiered tray. I had ordered the Compass Rose Tea Service.

The **China Oolong** tea would be perfect on a cold

day. (Oolong, which is a semi-fermented tea, means
dragon" in Chinese.) I decorated the small currant scone
ith Dickensen's strawberry preserves and "Devonshire
sauce," which is actually a mixture of sour cream and brown
sugar. Other teas (by HARNEY & SONS) include **Darjeeling,
Earl Grey** (regular and decaf), **English Breakfast, Gunpowder
Green, Hot Cinnamon Spice, Jasmine** (which is perfumed
with fresh flowers), **Lapsang Souchong, Orange Pekoe,** and
Russian Caravan. Chamomile and Peppermint are the herbal
teas.

On to the three generous finger sandwiches—smoked
salmon on a sourdough baguette, avocado and artichoke hearts
on marbled light and dark rye, and turkey on a small piece of
toast. After cleaning my Shenango plate of everything but its
leaves and flowers, I reached into the bowl of about half a
dozen fresh strawberries, took a juicy red one, and dipped it
into the remaining Devonshire sauce.

What would afternoon tea be without the sweets?
These came in the form of a blueberry tart, an almond petit
four, and a miniature cream horn. Blueberries toppled as I
poked the tart with my fork.

Afternoon Delicacies (such as Baba Ghannouj) and
Caviar are also offered. Spirits are available from the bar.
Frozen vodka is served at one's table from a block of ice.

Those meeting others at The Compass Rose may want
to follow San Francisco custom and rendezvous at the antique
Viennese Magneta grandfather clock in the lobby. But don't
be late!—the clock keeps perfect time.

ST. FRANCIS HOTEL
335 Powell Street (at Geary)
San Francisco, CA 94102

Phone	**(415) 397-7000, hotel; (415) 774-0167, afternoon tea reservations**
Web	**http://www.westin.com**
Hours	**Every day, 3:00 p.m.–5:00 p.m.**

Transport	* From Powell and Market, walk up Powell Street three blocks to Union Square. * From Fisherman's Wharf, take Powell cable car to Union Square.
Price	
Established	Hotel, 1904, the interior of which was destroyed by fire during the 1906 earthquake. Afternoon tea has been served in The Terrace Room since 1980, and in The Compass Rose since 1982.

COMPASS ROSE ROYAL TEA
COMPASS ROSE TEA SERVICE
A LA CARTE SELECTION
CAVIAR
AFTERNOON DELICACIES
SPARKLING WINES AND CHAMPAGNES

*Should I, after tea and cakes and ices,
Have the strength to force the moment to its crisis?*

T. S. Eliot (1888–1965)
The Love Song of J. Alfred Prufrock

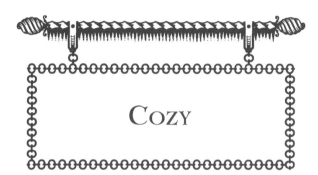

Cozy

THE BUTLER'S PANTRY
Authentic English Tearoom

Female bonding occurs over teacups. Heart-to-hearts. Two women at the next table were discussing everything from kindergartens to bellydancing. Their words poured out in a flurry of rapport, interrupted only by laughter, sips of tea, and thoughtful munches of finger sandwiches.

I unfolded my white cloth napkin, which was in the shape of a tuxedo jacket. (In keeping with the tearoom's theme, Hobbs, the lifesize statue of a butler, had already greeted me at the door.) Glass-topped tables, straight-backed chairs, and royal blue-and-yellow wallpaper lent an air of elegance and order. Just over my shoulder loomed a large, black-and-white illustration titled, *Their Royal Highnesses, The Duke and Duchess of York, Chapel Royal, St. James, July 6, 1893.*

According to the menu, the five afternoon teas—the Queen Mary, Queen Lucy, Queen Antoinette, Queen Frances, and Queen Josephine—are "dedicated to the owner's mother and her mother's four sisters for their strength, unity, and devotion to one another. Royalty doesn't come in any better way than family."

I selected the Queen Lucy with **Watermelon** tea. The three-tiered, sterling silver tray was laden with fruited scones (cranberry and orange) accompanied by lemon curd, strawberry preserves, and double Devon clotted cream; egg and chive finger sandwiches; hors d'oeuvres (quiche, spanakopita, and meat pasty); and assorted sweets (petit four, dainty meringue pie, and a napoleon). However, due to the chef's creativity, be advised that the type of scones, hors d'oeuvres, and sweets keeps changing.

Four dozen or so different teas, representing a hodgepodge of purveyors, among them TAYLORS OF HARROGATE, include other flavored teas, like **Peach** and **Vanilla**; black teas **Afternoon Darjeeling, Earl Grey, English Breakfast, Fine Assam, Irish Blend, Russian Style** and **Yorkshire Gold;** green teas **Gunpowder** and **Japanese Cherry;** and tisanes, such as **Chamomile** and **Rose Hips.**

The Butler's Pantry, originally owned by an English

couple, is now run by Becky Bonetti, who has brought out the gold flatware and filled the place with silk flowers. The flower arrangements may be purchased in the gift shop, along with tea-related books and accessories—everything from bone china teacups to sugar tongs.

Children's Teas feature the year-round Teddy Bear Tea (raspberry fizz or choice of tea, scones with preserves, peanut butter and jelly tea sandwiches, teapot cookies) and the Cotton Tail Tea (strawberry fizz or choice of tea, bologna and cheese tea sandwiches, scones and preserves, carrot cake).

No butlers here (except for Hobbs)—just nice folks. After a few cups, you'll even forget the mini-mall setting in the shadow of Starbucks. Be sure to visit the shops on nearby Main and State Streets.

THE BUTLER'S PANTRY
305 2nd Street
Los Altos, CA 94022

Phone	(650) 941-9676
Hours	Tuesday–Sunday, 11:00 a.m.–4:00 p.m. Closed Monday
Transport	From San Francisco by car, take Highway 280 south. Exit El Monte Road, going east (away from mountains). At fourth stoplight turn left on Foothill Expressway. At second stoplight turn right on Main Street. Continue on two blocks. Turn right on Second Street.
Price	🫖 🫖 🫖 *Credit cards and checks accepted*
Established	1993

QUEENS MARY, LUCY, ANTOINETTE,
    FRANCES, AND JOSEPHINE AFTERNOON TEA PLATES
CORNISH PASTY, WELSH RAREBIT, SHEPHERD'S PIE
TEDDY BEAR TEA AND COTTON TAIL TEA (FOR CHILDREN)

THE ENGLISH ROSE

This is a no-nonsense tearoom/restaurant, where the English feel at home. Big band music of the '30s and '40s plays, while proprietress Marilyn Sheppard dutifully serves BIGELOW, FARMER BROTHERS, and CELESTIAL SEASONINGS teas to her customers, none of whom are snobs about tea bags. All eleven tables are decked out in rose print tablecloths and laminated lace placemats. Roses, in one form or another, are everywhere.

Marilyn Sheppard was born in Middlesex, England. Before opening The English Rose, she and her aunt, Joyce Thomas (along with present owner, Susan Hayward) ran The Village Green in El Grenada, which was the first of the cozy tearooms of the Bay Area.

My teapot seemed demure, brewing **Orange Pekoe** (the name of which refers to the size and quality of the leaf, rather than its flavor) under its cozy. I glanced behind me at the fading portraits of the Prince and Princess of Wales, the Beefeater, and—could it be?—a troll doll. I read the poem by Helen Forsyth, printed on the back of the menu, which ends "...that which has placed you all others above,/Emblem of England and Symbol of love." Nearby, copies of the *Union Jack* (America's only national British newspaper) fluttered.

There is something decidedly kitschy and un-selfconscious about The English Rose (which has been voted "Best Authentic Teatime" by the *San Francisco Bay Guardian*). Its festive green garlands woven with pink pearls, pictures of unassuming village scenes (titled *Hunter's Inn*, *Roses and Larkspur*, *Departure of the Stag*), and handpainted bone china plates of, for example, the Fab Four, suggest an authenticity created over time that cannot be easily duplicated.

I ordered the Teaplate rather than the Devon Tea. Other "fayre" includes Shepherd's Pie, Banger and Onion Sandwich, and Rumbledethumps (potatoes fried with cabbage and onions). Ale—Stout, Cider, or Watney's—is also served. The tea selection is made up of old standards **Earl Grey** (regular and decaf) and **English Breakfast**, as well as a variety of herbal teas, among them **Black Currant, Licorice,** and **Strawberry**

Tea for Two at The English Rose

Mango.

Sausage with a frilled toothpick announced the arrival of my cornucopian Teaplate. Accompanying the sausage was a sandwich (in my case, cream cheese and cucumber), scone, crumpet, shortbread, chocolate cake, banana-pineapple cake, jam tart, and a raisin pastry. Everything but the crumpet was homemade. (Other sandwich choices include salmon and cucumber, cheese and chutney, cheese and tomato, and ham.)

Thin white crustless bread was cut into triangles. The scone was served *sans* clotted cream. (A "mock" clotted cream is available à la carte.) The tea was piping hot. I was fast becoming enamored of the shortbread and chocolate cake. I ate, and ate, and ate... It was quite a filling meal.

THE ENGLISH ROSE
663 Laurel Street
San Carlos, CA 94070

Phone	**(650) 595-5549**
Hours	**Tuesday–Saturday, 9:00 a.m.–3:30 p.m.** **(Last order by 3:00 p.m.)** **Closed Sunday and Monday**
Transport	**CalTrain to San Carlos Station. Cross El Camino Real and walk up San Carlos Avenue one block to Laurel. Turn left on Laurel. Fascinating shops nearby include Laurel Street Antiques & Collectibles and Mad About Dolls.**
Price	*Checks accepted. No credit cards*
Established	**1983**

TEAPLATE
DEVON TEA
A LA CARTE ENGLISH SANDWICHES
SHEPHERD'S PIE, RUMBLEDETHUMPS
ALE

The Garden Grill

The down-to-earth Garden Gril｡
eating and drinking establishments of O｡
proprietress Jessica Relinque lived for m
there's a bountiful flower garden, which ｡
on otherwise nondescript Alma Street. (
and instead of finding yourself inside a q   ...ｅ ｌearoom,
as you might expect, you're greeted by the mahogany-and-
copper world of The Red Terrier Public House, with its
grandfather clock, circular Inglenook fireplace, and dartboard.
Above the bar, which serves John Courage, Abbot, Bass, Red
Hook, and Harp on tap, span the cathedral-like Norman arches
of an extensive wine library. And then there's Ray Rastislav,
Jessica's father, who helps out around The Garden Grill as
needed. Born in Siberia, he is a friendly, engaging man with
many stories to tell.

In the restaurant area, where tea is served, Old English
tapestries grace the walls. I was seated in a carved wooden
rush chair that was fit for a hobbit. In one corner, a hutch was
filled with tea paraphernalia such as a toast caddy, and ceramic
Staffordshire dogs. Pale tulip sconces provided some
illumination for pondering the menu. Tea may also be taken
on the patio in the shade of a sprawling oak tree. There the
stone floor, fountains, and namesake grill, all surrounded by
a dark brown fence, offer one a cloistered sense of privacy.

Spirited background Celtic music — hammered
dulcimers, etc. — set the mood for afternoon tea. The teas, all
loose and ranging from TWININGS to PEET'S, usually feature
Earl Grey, English Breakfast, and **Darjeeling**, though the
choice is ever-changing. After a few strong cups of TAYLORS
OF HARROGATE **House Blend**, I felt the urge to get up and
do a jig, or perhaps a clumsy version of the Highland Fling.
Thankfully, the two-tiered tray arrived instead.

The Compleat Tea was a feast. The large, well-risen
scone was served with ruby-colored jam (strawberry or
raspberry) and Jessica Relinque's "clotted cream concoction,"
which, she insists, is superior to the imported variety. The tea
sandwiches upon my Bauscher Weiden plate included

gg and watercress, deviled ham, curried chicken moked salmon mousse, and my favorite, cheese and ey.

The pastries, jams, and even the thin tea sandwich breads, are all the creations of Pastry Chef Brian Victor. His culinary artfulness, influenced by the traditions of Europe, did not go unappreciated. Take, for instance, the chocolate Othello's cake with custard filling. The dreamy almond Tosca. Or the prim little tea cookie with dribbles of chocolate calligraphy written across its face. I'm afraid these are sweets meant for fighting over, rather than willingly sharing.

The Tea Party (for four or more) features miniature Cornish pasties, assorted tea sandwiches, scones with clotted cream and jam, cheddar cheese and tomato tartlets, mixed greens, tea cakes, and, of course, a pot of tea.

For those with a voracious sweet-tooth, The Garden Grill Cookie Plate, Chocolate-Apricot Soufflé Cake, Lemon Flummery, Frozen Hazelnut Praline Gateau, Sherry Trifle, and a Dessert of the Day, are available à la carte.

Jessica and her husband, José Luis Relinque, also run The Iberia Spanish restaurant in Portola Valley. Adjacent to The Garden Grill, their Rock of Gibraltar gourmet shop features homemade scones, Irish soda breads, and pastries, as well as both English and Spanish products.

THE GARDEN GRILL
1026 Alma Street (between Oak Grove and Ravenswood)
Menlo Park, CA 94025

Phone   **(650) 325-8981**

Hours   **Afternoon tea, Monday–Saturday, 3:00 p.m.–5:00 p.m.**
                 Restaurant serves lunch Monday–Friday, 11:30 a.m.–2:30 p.m., and dinner every night from 5:30 p.m. Separate pub menu from opening to closing time.

Transport   **CalTrain to Menlo Park Station. Facing north, walk parallel to train tracks a short**

THE GARDEN GRILL

The down-to-earth Garden Grill is fashioned after the eating and drinking establishments of Oxford, England, where proprietress Jessica Relinque lived for many years. Out front, there's a bountiful flower garden, which appears like a mirage on otherwise nondescript Alma Street. Open the front door, and instead of finding yourself inside a quaint little tearoom, as you might expect, you're greeted by the mahogany-and-copper world of The Red Terrier Public House, with its grandfather clock, circular Inglenook fireplace, and dartboard. Above the bar, which serves John Courage, Abbot, Bass, Red Hook, and Harp on tap, span the cathedral-like Norman arches of an extensive wine library. And then there's Ray Rastislav, Jessica's father, who helps out around The Garden Grill as needed. Born in Siberia, he is a friendly, engaging man with many stories to tell.

In the restaurant area, where tea is served, Old English tapestries grace the walls. I was seated in a carved wooden rush chair that was fit for a hobbit. In one corner, a hutch was filled with tea paraphernalia such as a toast caddy, and ceramic Staffordshire dogs. Pale tulip sconces provided some illumination for pondering the menu. Tea may also be taken on the patio in the shade of a sprawling oak tree. There the stone floor, fountains, and namesake grill, all surrounded by a dark brown fence, offer one a cloistered sense of privacy.

Spirited background Celtic music — hammered dulcimers, etc. — set the mood for afternoon tea. The teas, all loose and ranging from TWININGS to PEET'S, usually feature **Earl Grey, English Breakfast,** and **Darjeeling**, though the choice is ever-changing. After a few strong cups of TAYLORS OF HARROGATE **House Blend**, I felt the urge to get up and do a jig, or perhaps a clumsy version of the Highland Fling. Thankfully, the two-tiered tray arrived instead.

The Compleat Tea was a feast. The large, well-risen scone was served with ruby-colored jam (strawberry or raspberry) and Jessica Relinque's "clotted cream concoction," which, she insists, is superior to the imported variety. The tea sandwiches upon my Bauscher Weiden plate included cucumber, egg and watercress, deviled ham, curried chicken spread, smoked salmon mousse, and my favorite, cheese and chutney. The pastries, jams, and even the thin tea sandwich breads, are all the creations of Pastry Chef Brian Victor. His culinary artfulness, influenced by the traditions of Europe, did not go unappreciated. Take, for instance, the chocolate Othello's cake with custard filling. The dreamy almond Tosca. Or the prim little tea cookie with dribbles of chocolate calligraphy written across its face. I'm afraid these are sweets meant for fighting over, rather than willingly sharing.

The Tea Party (for four or more) features miniature Cornish pasties, assorted tea sandwiches, scones with clotted cream and jam, cheddar cheese and tomato tartlets, mixed greens, tea cakes, and, of course, a pot of tea.

For those with a voracious sweet-tooth, The Garden Grill Cookie Plate, Chocolate-Apricot Soufflé Cake, Lemon Flummery, Frozen Hazelnut Praline Gateau, Sherry Trifle, and a Dessert of the Day, are available à la carte.

Jessica and her husband, José Luis Relinque, also run The Iberia Spanish restaurant in Portola Valley. Adjacent to The Garden Grill, their Rock of Gibraltar gourmet shop features homemade scones, Irish soda breads, and pastries, as well as both English and Spanish products.

THE GARDEN GRILL
1026 Alma Street (between Oak Grove and Ravenswood)
Menlo Park, CA 94025

Phone   (650) 325-8981

Hours   Afternoon tea, Monday–Saturday, 3:00 p.m.–5:00 p.m.
                  Restaurant serves lunch Monday–Friday, 11:30 a.m.–2:30 p.m., and dinner every night from 5:30 p.m. Separate pub menu from opening to closing time.

Transport   CalTrain to Menlo Park Station. Facing north, walk parallel to train tracks a short

distance. Turn right on Oak Grove. Cross tracks. Turn right on Alma Street. (It is also possible to reach The Garden Grill by facing south and turning left on Ravenswood). Be sure to visit nearby Kepler's Books.

Price

Credit cards and checks accepted

Established

Restaurant, 1988. Afternoon tea served since 1990

THE COMPLEAT TEA
THE CREAM TEA
THE TEA PARTY
A LA CARTE DESSERTS
SHERRIES AND PORTS
WINES
BRITISH DRAFT BEERS

*"Come, little cottage girl, you seem
To want my cup of tea;
And will you take a little cream?
Now tell the truth to me."*

*She had a rustic, woodland grin
Her cheek was soft as silk,
And she replied, "Sir, please put in
A little drop of milk."*

Barry Pain (1864–1928)
The Poets at Tea: Wordsworth

KING GEORGE HOTEL
WINDSOR TEAROOM

Alas, the rate for a single room at the King George is no longer just a dollar a night, as it was when the hotel first opened in 1914. Fortunately, though, the service and sense of hospitality at this small establishment have remained much the same. The Windsor (formerly known as the Bread & Honey) is a comfortable place, a hideaway of sorts, where guests of the hotel, shoppers, and theatre-goers alike can escape from the "madding crowd."

Located on the mezzanine, the tearoom is reached by a spiral marble staircase (or elevator) and overlooks the goings-on of the chandeliered lobby. Written across the grandfather clock's face are the words *tempus fugit* (time flies) — ironic, because, upon inspection, I discovered that its hands were motionless.

The eye-following portrait of Queen Elizabeth (shown wearing gown and tiara), tins of tea upon the sideboard, souvenir statue of a guard, draped Union Jack, and tile trivets of dogs and hunt scenes give the hotel's many British guests the perhaps not-unsurreal feeling of a home-away-from-home. Multitudes of prim pink roses decorate the gold-rimmed bone china by Hudson Middleton.

The High Tea, technically an afternoon tea, or, if you will, a low tea, is nevertheless a filling meal of tea and scones, two sandwiches (choose from cucumber and cream cheese, roast beef and horseradish, smoked turkey, honey roast ham, and cheddar cheese and tomato) two salads (potato and seafood), and cookies (or "biscuits," as the British say).

I had the Devonshire Cream Tea — two hefty raisin scones, clotted cream, strawberry jam, and a pot of **Assam**. The garnish was a curious mound of grapes (painstakingly sculpted in the shape of stars), blueberries, and kiwi. I was surprised to learn, as I bit into a warm, chewy scone, that the scones, clotted cream, tea, and cookies are all imported from England. (Interestingly, the jam hails from California.)

Other items on the menu combine British staples such as cheeses, fruit, and cream crackers. The Duck Pâté is served

King George Advertisement, circa 1914

with toast and butter. Soup & Sarnies (small tea-style sandwiches) are another possibility. Sweets include Hot Apple Pie and Ice Cream with Cadbury's Chocolate, and Bakewell Tarts and Double Devon Cream.

The TAYLORS OF HARROGATE tea list features several black teas, such as **Earl Grey** and **English Breakfast** (both regular and decaf), **Special Darjeeling** and **Yorkshire Gold,** flavored teas (**Apple, Apricot, Black Currant, Christmas Blend, Mango, Passion Fruit,** and **Peach**), and tisanes (**Chamomile, Hibiscus, Peppermint,** and **Rosehips**).

A pianist once entertained tea-drinkers here, but on the day I visited, the piano (which has since disappeared) remained agonizingly silent; instead, piped-in Vivaldi could be heard.

Note the old photograph of the King George hanging above one of the tables, a stoical reminder of the past.

KING GEORGE HOTEL
334 Mason Street (at Geary)
San Francisco, CA 94102

Phone	**(415) 781-5050, hotel; 283-4TEA, afternoon tea reservations**
Web	**http://www.kinggeorge.com**
Hours	**Wednesday–Sunday, 3:00 p.m.–6:30 p.m. Closed Monday and Tuesday**
Transport	**From Powell and Market, walk up Powell Street three blocks to Union Square. Turn left on Geary and walk one block to Mason.**
Price	🫖 🫖 🫖 *Credit cards and checks accepted*
Established	**Hotel, 1914. A restaurant, piano bar, and the Bread & Honey Tearoom have occupied the mezzanine since the hotel opened. Windsor Tearoom, 1997**

HIGH TEA
DEVONSHIRE CREAM TEA
THREE CHEESE PLOUGHSHARES
CHEESE AND FRESH FRUIT PLATTER
PATÉ AND TOAST
HOT TOASTED CRUMPETS WITH PATÉ
SOUPS AND SARNIES
CAKES AND COOKIES

Teas,

Where small talk dies in agonies.

Percy Bysshe Shelley (1792–1822)
Peter Bell the Third

LADY PIERREPONT'S
Heirlooms & Edibles

Karen Strange, proprietress of Lady Pierrepont's, is a tall, swanlike woman with a penchant for old cookbooks and cooking. She and husband Herb have created a typically English, village-style, very cozy tearoom, which is recognized as one of *the* tearooms of the Bay Area.

This tearoom is located on the main floor of a two-story house, not far from a pub called Paddy Flynn's and the pink rose bushes of the Burlingame train station. Built in 1908, and made into apartments after World War II, it was once the home of Emile Maisson, a retired sea captain. Despite renovations (painting the barn-red structure grey-green and burgundy and planting a lawn in place of cement), the plaque that Emile Maisson had installed in memory of his wife remains. Today, when something creaks or falls, Karen Strange thinks, "I guess the Captain is about."

I began my visit by navigating through the labyrinthine gift shop of mostly English products. Tins of Fortnum & Mason tea, jellies and curds, Bird's custard powder, and Walker's shortbread, gave way to Pimpernel coasters of castles and gardens, a small beanbag frog from Liberty's, and a hodgepodge of pretty bone china.

Fearing that, by the simple act of breathing, I might accidentally break something, I headed straight for the tearoom and ordered the Traditional Afternoon Tea. (Other options are the Cream Tea and the Cheese Tea, which features English and French cheeses, biscuits, fresh fruit, nuts, and a Branston pickle.) Oddly, the only tea choice here is FORTNUM & MASON **Royal Blend** (Ceylon and India teas), however it is strong enough to hold its own with even the lunchtime menu of, say, Welsh Rarebit or Bangers and Mash.

I was noting the pink-and-green color scheme—how the cozies perfectly match the curtains—when Herb Strange himself approached. Soon I was learning about the family manor, Thoresby Hall, which is located in Sherwood Forest, and James Pierrepont (founder of Yale), and Bluestocking Lady Mary Pierrepont (with whom Alexander Pope was infatuated).

Did I mention William the Conqueror, his 25th great-grandfather? The Pierrepont history is a complex and intriguing one.

The green tablecloths and napkins now seemed linked with the green of Sherwood Forest; the fireplace and wood-beamed ceiling — even the small vase of pink and white carnations — evoked another place and time.

While debutantes traditionally flock to the Palace Hotel for their Cotillion Balls, the Brownies of Burlingame come to Lady Pierrepont's to earn their etiquette badges. According to Karen Strange, the out-of-uniform Brownies conduct themselves like "little ladies."

"All desserts are homemade on the premises," the menu states. I was eager to try the pecan tart, because, as Herb Strange had confided, when his wife serves this sweet at Christmas parties, "People devour them." But first, I would have to wade through the currant scone with fresh heavy cream and strawberry jam, the cucumber and curried turkey sandwiches....

Soon my plate was bare but for a lemon square with a nice thick crust, a wholemeal shortbread triangle, a round of chocolate bourbon cake — and the pecan tart. I poured myself another cup of tea, in anticipation.

LADY PIERREPONT'S
1205 Howard Avenue
Burlingame, CA 94010

Phone	(650) 342-6065
Hours	Afternoon tea, Tuesday–Saturday, 3:00 p.m.–4:30 p.m. Restaurant serves morning coffee Tuesday–Saturday, 10:00 a.m.–11:00 a.m. and lunch Tuesday–Saturday, 11:30 a.m.–2:00 p.m. Closed Sunday and Monday
Transport	CalTrain to Burlingame Station. Turn left on California Drive and walk one block. Turn right on Howard Avenue.

Price

Credit cards and checks accepted

Established 1990

TRADITIONAL AFTERNOON TEA
CHEESE TEA
CREAM TEA
A LA CARTE DESSERTS

The cosy fire is bright and gay,
The merry kettle boils away
And hums a cheerful song.
I sing the saucer and the cup;
Pray, Mary, fill the teapot up,
And do not make it strong.

Pour, varlet, pour the water,
The water steaming hot!
A spoonful for each man of us,
Another for the pot!

Barry Pain (1864–1928)
The Poets at Tea: Wordsworth and Macaulay

LISA'S TEA TREASURES
Tearoom & Gift Parlour

"I feel like I've stepped into another era," a woman gasped.

This Victorian-style tearoom, with its plush, dusty-rose carpet, lace curtains, and antique reproduction pieces, often has such an effect on people. The fantasy is omnipresent, cause for a case of the vapours sometimes.

Each table is set with Royal Albert bone china, a cookie jar of ginger snaps, and a white porcelain bell, meant for conjuring your waitress. She would be the one dressed in a high-collared black frock, pinafore, with a doily-like bonnet on her head.

The menu's theme is "afternoon tea times from around the world." Each selection is matched with a LISA'S TEA TREASURES tea: The Duchess' Delight with **Boysenberry** tea; Louis XIV's Favorite, **Blackberry Jasmine**; My Lady's Respite, **Earl Grey**; The Summer Regatta, **Peach**; The Venetian's Romance, **Amaretto**; The Marquis' Light Delight (fat-free) with a **Cranberry Orange** tisane; and The Court Jester's Surprise (for children) is paired with **Watermelon Berry**.

My Lady's Respite appealed, in the form of a plate of small sandwiches — salmon, chicken tarragon, pesto, cucumber, and ham and honey mustard (the latter on marbled bread) — a nutty scone with double Devon clotted cream, tea gelée, and lemon curd, a spicy herb soufflé, raspberry fingerprint cookie, bite-sized cheesecake, and a marvelous carrot cake petit four. The Earl Grey tea was scented with lavender and rose petals.

Respite, indeed. Afterwards, I sat sipping tea, listening to the romantic whistling of the train as it arrived at, and departed from, the nearby station. Though some of the more jaded among us may deem Lisa's Tea Treasures' theatrical approach to preciousness a bit "over the top," by now I was feeling, not only pampered, well-sated, and civilized, but — dare I admit it? — rather like a Victorian lady.

TEA PRINCESS teas (sold loose-leaf or in sachets) include exclusive blends such as **The Contessa's Jewel, King**

Ludwig's Wish, and **The Rajah's Prize**. The complete tea list is quite extensive. The categories are Classic Tea Blends; Ancient & Old World Tea Blends; China Teas; Japan, South American, African and Caucasus Teas; South Pacific, Ceylon, and Formosa Teas; Indian Teas; Chai Blends; Herbal Tisanes and Frutta Tea Blends; Treasured Teas; Iced Teas; Fantasy Teas; and Celebration Teas.

At the time of this writing, there are seven licensed Lisa's Tea Treasures. Each (like this one, which is run by proprietress Roberta Oswald), reflects the vision of founder Lisa Strauss, a former inhabitant of the high-tech world, who was inspired to create the first tearoom after experiencing an especially nostalgic afternoon tea at Raffles Hotel in Singapore.

The Gift Parlour brims with treasures such as sealing wax, Sadler's heirloom teapots, and a wicker hamper containing a miniature tea set, which is presumably intended for dolls.

Some may prefer to take their tea in The Hunt Parlor, an intimate, red-and-green room, with stately mirror and fireplace, which adjoins the tearoom proper.

LISA'S TEA TREASURES
1145 Merrill Street
Menlo Park, CA 94025

other Bay Area locations:
1875 South Bascom Ave., Campbell, CA 95008 (408) 371-7377
330 North Santa Cruz Ave., Los Gatos, CA 95030 (408) 395-8327
71 Lafayette Circle, Lafayette, CA 94549 (510) 283-2226

Phone	**(650) 326-8327**
Web	**http://www.lisasteas.com**
Hours	**Tuesday–Sunday seatings at 11:30 a.m., 2:00 p.m., and 4:00 p.m.** **Closed Monday and holidays**
Transport	**CalTrain to Menlo Park Station. Face west. Tearoom is located right across the street. Be sure to visit nearby Kepler's Books.**

Price	*Credit cards and checks accepted*
Established	**Original Lisa's Tea Treasures, 1988. Menlo Park tearoom, 1994**

Menu

THE DUCHESS' DELIGHT
MY LADY'S RESPITE
THE SUMMER REGATA
THE VENETIAN'S ROMANCE
LOUIS XIV'S FAVORITE
THE MARQUIS' LIGHT DELIGHT
THE COURT JESTER'S SURPRISE (FOR CHILDREN)
LIGHT AFTERNOON TEA DELIGHTS

I raised to my lips a spoonful of the cake...a shudder ran through my whole body and I stopped, intent upon the extraordinary changes that were taking place....

Marcel Proust (1871–1922)
Remembrance of Things Past

LOVEJOY'S
Antiques & Tearoom

Lovejoy's is a quirky neighborhood tearoom that serves authentic English tearoom "fayre." One window looks out at busy Church Street, while others, which are dressed deceptively in floral-patterned curtains, view pastoral trompe l'oeil scenes of streams and hillsides. In fact, after a few cups of tea, one tends to forget that this is *not* an English cottage. Maybe it's the lacy tablecloths, wood beams, the hearth and mantle. When I visited, it didn't take long before I felt as though I'd been transported, if only for a moment, "across the pond."

Locals may recall the time before Lovejoy's, when the storefront was occupied by a fortune teller's salon. The tearoom itself was named after Lovejoy, a fictional antique dealer with a knack for becoming involved in mysteries. New proprietresses, friends Terri Harte and Tricia Hollenberg (who hail from Ireland and Scotland, respectively), continue the tradition set by Lovejoy's original owners by offering for sale antique teacups and saucers, teas, and Devonshire clotted cream. Ms. Hollenberg, a gifted psychic, gives Tarot readings (either by appointment or drop-by). In the spirit of research, I shuffled the deck, and found her heartfelt words to be both accurate and inspiring.

The surprisingly substantial Light Tea consists of a pot of **Tea Room Blend**, a sandwich (arranged in four triangles), scones, and a petite dessert. Add another sandwich and two salads (coleslaw and mixed greens), and you have the makings of the High Tea. The sandwich selection is vast—from cucumber and cream cheese, roast beef with horseradish, to chicken and asparagus, to name just a few.

I was in the mood for the Cream Tea. Two well-risen raisin scones (prepared by a local baker) were served with double Devon clotted cream and strawberry preserves. Tea was poured from a Brown Betty teapot into my waiting teacup, which was of a pale blue, with a pattern of exotic birds perched hither and thither. A word about the **Tea Room Blend** (available regular and decaf), which accompanies the Cream, Light, and High Teas: A blend of malty Assam, Ceylon, and

The Table is Set for Tea at Lovejoy's

The Magic Mirror

East African teas, it has, on occasion, been voted the Best Cup of Tea in England.

Lovejoy's pours only TAYLORS OF HARROGATE teas: **Afternoon Darjeeling, Earl Grey, English Breakfast, Single-Estate Ceylon,** and **Yorkshire Gold**. The tisanes, or fruit infusions, are **Chamomile, Peppermint,** and **Rose Hip Hibiscus**; the flavored teas are **Apple, Apricot, Black Currant, Mango, Passion Fruit,** and **Peach**. Iced tea is also served.

Baby's first tea! I thought, glancing at the family in the corner. The baby, oblivious to the finer points of the tea experience, smiled and gurgled and cooed from his place on the red velvet settee. That is, until he became frightened by the bouquet of bright pink carnations—and then he cried. His cry was quite shrill, and I worried that teacups would shatter. I dabbed my mouth politely while Father passed him to Mother, who stood, and patted the infant's heaving back, but to no avail. Finally, in between much pacing, she held him before an antique mirror, and thankfully he was soon consoled by his own reflection.

The above scene was tolerated well by Terri Harte, herself a mother of three. Resembling a modern-day Cinderella in her lacy blouse and flowing green satin skirt as she tended her tables, it became clear to me why so many flock here—it simply feels like home.

Lovejoy's is near a shop called Do Dah Days, a Pandora's Box of eccentric collectibles. A walk along 24th Street (heading west) is recommended.

LOVEJOY'S
1195 Church Street (at 24th Street)
San Francisco, CA 94114

Phone   **(415) 648-5895**

Hours   **Monday–Friday, 11:00 a.m.–7:00 p.m.**
              Saturday and Sunday, 10:30 a.m.–7:00 p.m.

Transport   **J-Church streetcar**

Price

Checks accepted; no credit cards

Established   1994

HIGH TEA
LIGHT TEA
CREAM TEA
WEE TEA (FOR CHILDREN)
TEA SANDWICHES
TOASTED CRUMPETS
FRUITED SCONES
PLOUGHMAN'S LUNCH
SAVORY BEEF OR CURRIED CHICKEN PASTY
THREE SAUSAGE ROLLS

Polly, put the kettle on, we'll all have tea.

Charles Dickens (1812–1870)
Barnaby Rudge

TAL-Y-TARA
Tea & Polo Shoppe

Ethereal harp music gre⟨⟩
Tal-y-Tara. But that was only th⟨⟩
served a cozied pot of **Blue La⟨⟩**
chip scone, Sarah Meakin (dau⟨⟩
Melba) returned to her harp and, ⟨⟩
voice serenaded me with "Come O'er the Sea, ⟨⟩
song. I was charmed, lost in an intercontinental daydream.
My gaze passed from the French oak mantle jammed with
knick-knacks, along the Aladdin-like carpets, to the beckoning
green of the patio garden (where tea may also be taken).

My table mat, which depicted a classic hunt scene
(captioned *The Meeting of her Majesty's Stag Hounds on Ascot
Heath*), drew my attention to the fact that Tal-y-Tara is a
tearoom with a decidedly equestrian twist. Witness the retail
hodgepodge of riding breeches, boots, gloves, whips,
harnesses, bridles, and bits—not to mention the boxes of
"Sweet Lumps," and the weathered antique carriage in the
storefront window.

Their specialty is Motorloaf, a small loaf of homemade
molasses-nut bread which has been hollowed out, its crustless
center transformed into six tasty finger sandwiches (cream
cheese and cucumber, cream cheese and watercress, turkey,
ham, cheese and chutney, egg salad and capers) which are
then fitted back inside the bread shell and, as if that were not
enough, garnished with fruit. The recipe dates back to the early
1900s, when Motorloaf was thought to be the ideal picnic food
to take along on a Sunday drive.

Scones and crumpets are always a temptation,
especially when the clotted cream involved is the real thing,
imported from Devon. TWININGS, JACKSONS OF
PICCADILLY, WHITTARD OF CHELSEA, and TY·PHOO are
just some of the British teas in stock, along with MCGRATH
BROTHERS from Ireland. Unusual teas, such as SILK ROAD
TEAS **Green Sea Anemone**, are also offered.

Tea is made "the correct way"—a subject about which
Hugh Meakin is adamant. First, while fresh, cold water is being

olling boil in the kettle*, the teapot is doused
ater. About one teaspoon of loose-leaf tea per
d one for the pot, is added to the preheated teapot.
ng water is then poured over the leaves, and the teapot
ckly covered and nestled in its cozy. The tea is steeped
ut three to five minutes — or, in the words of a Sir Kenelm
igby, "The water is to remain upon it no longer than whiles
you can say the Misere Psalm very leisurely." Note: Green
teas require water that is not quite boiled, and they should
not steep as long.

At Tal-y-Tara, a genuine (if sometimes playful) sense
of hospitality is extended to each guest. This is a homey,
magical place — a bubble in time, of sorts — to which you'll want
to return again and again. (Those who love both tea *and* horses
may never want to leave.) It is also an ideal out-of-the-way
meeting spot for friends and business acquaintances.

Before creating Tal-y-Tara (Gaelic for "by the ancient
seat of the kings"), the Meakins ran the Waters Upton Tea
Room; that site is now occupied by a Walgreens. Hugh Meakin
himself is the great-grandson of James Meakin, of J & G Meakin
Pottery, which was founded in Britain in 1851. A quick peek
under my teacup revealed that this same china is in service
today at Tal-y-Tara.

*Tea experts agree that these variables are crucial:
Twice-boiled water results in flat tea.*

TAL-Y-TARA
**6439 California Street (at 27th Avenue)
San Francisco, CA 94121**

Phone   (415) 751-9275

Hours   Monday–Saturday, 10:00 a.m.–6:00 p.m.
Closed Sunday

Transport   1-California Muni bus

Price

Credit cards and checks accepted

Established   **Waters Upton, 1981. Tal-y-Tara, 1995**

THE MOTORLOAF (FOR TWO)
MOTORLOAF PLATE
MOTORLOAF BREAD
ENGLISH TRIFLE
SCONES
CRUMPETS

Thank God for tea!
What would the world do without tea?—how did it exist?
I am glad I was not born before tea.

Reverend Sydney Smith
Lady Holland's Memoir, 1855

THE VILLAGE GREEN

This family-run, English-style tearoom/restaurant is located between Princeton and Miramar, about five miles north of Half Moon Bay. Past the fire station, the hardware store, U-turn at the post office... The Village Green, which resembles a Tudor cottage, sports a Union Jack flag out front and window boxes full of an ever-changing array of flowers.

Inside, lace curtains hang in gentle drifts. The black tablecloths are splashed with a tea-inspired print, and the carpet is sand-colored. From some tables you can see the ocean. A demure Princess Anne, shown in portrait wearing a gown with puffed sleeves (rather than her preferred riding habit), gazes benevolently at tea-drinkers. Photos of the Royal Family, the Tower, the Thames, and Big Ben decorate the walls, along with a cricket tea towel, an actual cricket bat and pad, and a frayed cricket pennant.

I sat near a retired couple from Florida and ordered the Cream Tea. Though The Village Green has its share of regulars, many migrate here from other parts each year, such as New York, Baltimore, and Nevada City. The Hayward family themselves hail from Bath, England.

I liked the informality of The Village Green — the way waitress Heidi (daughter of proprietress Susan Hayward, who also runs the local dance school) swung open the screen door and shouted "Yoo-hoo!" to a neighbor. And I even enjoyed the three-bags-strong pot of **generic** FARMER BROTHERS tea, which Grandpa Hayward swears by. (**Herbal** teas and BIGELOW **Constant Comment** are also offered). The two raisin scones were especially tasty with homemade lemon curd, "clotted" cream (grated frozen sweet butter and heavy whipping cream), and mounds of raspberry jam.

The perfect "take-away" choice for a beach picnic is the Ploughman's Lunch and a few bottles of imported beer (such as Bass, Guinness Stout, Popes, and John Courage). One specialty is the Cornish Pasty, which, as the menu explains, "originated from the Cornish tin miners who devised a method of taking their meat, potatoes, and vegetables to work by wrapping it in pastry." Bubble & Squeak is a boiled, mixed, and fried cabbage-and-potato dish. Tea-time delicacies include English Trifle, Hot Fruit Crumble, Eccles Cake, Crumpets (described as "similar to English muffins, but with more holes"), Treacle Tarts, and Victorian Sandwich Cake. Cream sherry is available by the glass.

The gift nook features Crownford teapots, cozies, and assorted bone china. Jars of homemade lemon curd and Olde English salt and vinegar potato crisps are also for sale.

In feudal times, the village green was where bowmen practiced their archery; in the England of today, it is the site of celebrations such as cricket matches, May Day, and church fetes. El Granada's Village Green is where locals, and tourists alike, gather. It is the destination of schoolchildren on field trips, who come to learn about etiquette and culture—and who, though they invariably arrive disheveled and windswept, upon spotting the frilly tea cozies and white Gibson china, somehow manage to behave themselves, and rise to the occasion.

THE VILLAGE GREEN
89 Avenue Portola
El Granada, CA 94018

Phone   (650) 726-3690

Hours   Monday, Tuesday, Thursday, Friday, 9:00 a.m.–
               3:00 p.m.
               Saturday and Sunday, 9:00 a.m.–4:00 p.m.
               Closed Wednesday (and for a few weeks every
               summer)

Transport   From San Francisco by car, take Highway 1
               (Cabrillo Highway) south, past Devil's Slide.
               When you reach stoplights near Chinese
               Restaurant, turn left onto Capistrano.
               Immediately bear right along Avenue Alhambra.
               At the fork, continue to bear right along Obispo
               until you reach the fire station. Turn left at
               Avenue Portola.

Price   *Credit cards and checks accepted*

Established   **July 4, 1978**

TEAPLATE
CREAM TEA
CAKES AND TEA-TIME DELICACIES
PLOUGHMAN'S LUNCH
CORNISH PASTY
BUBBLE & SQUEAK
CREAM SHERRY
IMPORTED BEERS

*A woman is like a teabag—you can't tell how
strong she is until you put her in hot water.*

Nancy Reagan

OLD WORLD

GREEN GULCH FARM ZEN CENTER
SHUGETSUAN

A winding path leads to *Shugetsuan*, or Sowing the Moon Tea House. Nestled in a bucolic valley near the Pacific Ocean and overseen by the practicing Buddhists of the Green Gulch Farm Zen Center, the teahouse represents a point of calm and civility in an oft-hectic world. For this reason alone, a visit to *Shugetsuan* is well worth the journey.

Near a grove of bamboo, round stones dot the way past the *tsukubai* (stone water basin, traditionally used to cleanse one's hands and face before the tea ceremony), which was a gift from modern-day pilgrim, scholar, and author, Huston Smith. The teahouse was designed by Makoto Imai, a master shrine and teahouse builder, and its construction completed by master carpenter, Hiroshi Sakaguchi. Inside the finely crafted structure, an almost palpable sense of peace pervades.

After removing shoes and signing the guest book, the other guests and I politely regarded the small scroll, which hung on the wall of the waiting room. Though we admired its calligraphy, we knew not what it meant. Finally our host, Meiya Wender, a Zen priest, translated it for us: "The flower wears dewdrops like jewels. Its fragrance creates a pure heart."

Randall Weingarten, our gentle-spirited co-host, knelt beside her. Explaining the theme of the day's tea ceremony, which centered around the Japanese *Tanabata* celebration, or Star Festival, he told of a Chinese myth, in which a weaver and an ox-herder who have fallen in love are separated, only to be reunited once a year when they cross a bridge formed by the Milky Way. Like a child listening to a bedtime story, I felt my own cares and concerns slowly slipping away.

Next, for the purpose of making obeisance, we scooted into the tearoom. And I mean *scooted*. This, as Randall demonstrated, is accomplished on hands and knees. One by one, we all followed suit, though not without some giggles. That accomplished, our task now was to behave as good guests—that is, to receive the tea in the correct manner, and with gratitude.

This is not as easy as it seems. For instance, there are times to bow, and times to pardon oneself for drinking before the next person. (This last detail I remembered mid-gulp, as did a few others.) Each ritualized act is deep with meaning. For Westerners especially, the experience requires a subtle re-focusing of attention—a shift of mind and heart.

The *tokonoma*, or alcove, was graced by an arrangement of bright, summery flowers which were accented by wisps of eulalia grass. Behind the flowers hung a large scroll. Its message concerned "soft mind," or the attitude of being in the present moment rather than the "hard mind" way of wishing that one were somewhere else.

Tea was prepared and served with great care—from the dipping of the ladle into the hot water, the whisking of the **matcha** (powdered green tea), to the moment when the steaming bowl was set before one with a bow. All of these elements served to create a sense of timelessness and wonder.

A tasty, lime-green sweet (which resembled a lotus flower) was made of rice flour and lima beans, by Yamada Seika Confectionery in San Francisco. These creations vary according to theme and season; each is a work of art unto itself.

The heavenly tea, which is imported from Japan, had a faint woodsy taste. I sipped slowly from my blue-grey ceramic bowl, wanting to savor it.

"At this point in the ceremony, it is customary to socialize," said Randall cheerfully after Meiya had poured the last bowl of tea. His announcement was followed by silence. It seemed that it was enough just to be in the sanctuary of the teahouse, kneeling on the *tatami* (straw mat), or, in my case, glimpsing the swaying pine past the window's parted screen. Who wanted to break the silence, ruin the effect?

And so no one spoke. Instead, it seemed we strangers, brought together in the name of tea, were content to say nothing at all.

GREEN GULCH FARM ZEN CENTER
1601 Shoreline Highway
Sausalito, CA 94965

Phone   (415) 383-3134

Hours   Sunday Tea Gatherings are held once a month,
                1:30 p.m.–3:00 p.m., by reservation only. An
                introductory course, ongoing classes (in both the
                Urasenke and Omotesenke traditions), "A Day
                of Zen and Tea" workshop, and special tea
                gatherings are also offered.

Transport   From San Francisco by car, take Highway 101
                north to Stinson Beach exit. Continue to
                stoplight at the landmark Marin Oriental Rug
                House. Turn left onto Route 1. After about
                three miles, turn left at fork, heading towards
                Muir Beach. After about two more miles, you'll
                see the Green Gulch Farm driveway on your left.
                Park in lot, and walk along paved path to office.
                The teahouse is nearby.

Price

($15.00 per person, paid in advance)

Established   1972, Green Gulch Farm Zen Center. 1986,
                Shugetsuan (teahouse)

MATCHA
JAPANESE SWEET

Before you study Zen, a bowl is a bowl and tea is tea.
While you are studying Zen, a bowl is no longer a bowl and
tea is no longer tea.
After you've studied Zen, a bowl is a bowl again and tea is tea.

Zen saying

IMPERIAL TEA COURT

A brass monkey crouches in the window of the Imperial Tea Court, which has the distinction of being America's first traditional Chinese teahouse. Proprietors and tea masters Roy and Grace Fong (themselves the owners of several tea farms in their native China) purvey the finest Black, Green, Oolong, Pu-erh, Scented, and White teas. Guests are encouraged to "experience the tradition" as tea is sampled in a *gaiwan* (covered porcelain cup), or served in the *kung fu* style, in a small, unglazed Yixing teapot.

The electric kettle rumbled on the rosewood table as Morris, my tea initiator, revealed the dried brown leaves of the **Superior Yunnan Pu-erh**. He brought the small, handleless cup closer, encouraging me to sniff the bouquet. Next he added hot water, swirled, and then rinsed out the first blush of tea into a round tea drainer. The cup was refilled, and again, at his prompting, I sniffed, this time noticing the emanations of a bolder scent. I was instructed how to brush back the loose leaves with the lid and sip, while keeping the lid in place and balancing the cup and saucer in the palm of my hand. This seemed easy when Morris demonstrated it, but I found that the saucer slipped menacingly from the cup while my nose nudged the lid, thus tingeing my experience of tea nirvana with the fear that I would, in the process, scald myself. Finally, though, I was able to enjoy the brew. Pu-erh tea, which is known for its health benefits, tasted pleasantly dark and earthy.

Distracting me from this ritual were a dozen or so spirited Chinese men who occupied the back corner of the Imperial Tea Court — and their respective pet finches, canaries, and nightingales. The singing chorus of birds bobbed and swayed in ornamental wood and bamboo cages which were hung from the ceiling. The tea court was beginning to resemble an aviary.

As the men of the "Bird Club" cackled with laughter, I was reminded of the Greek men who sit in public squares, flicking worry beads. "What are they talking about?" I asked Morris over the din, to which he replied with a sigh, "Everything under the sun."

Kung fu is literally translated as "accomplished technique," or, in the words of Mr. Fong: *Kung fu applies to almost everything in life (not only to the martial arts)—anything that requires repetition, patience, and learned skill to achieve.*

Yixing teapots possess a curious appeal. Created by the potter Gong Chun, they were first enjoyed by members of the Ming Dynasty's royal court in the 16th century. Today they are still made from the same special purple clay of the Yixing region, as they were during Chun's time, and have earned a reputation for their brewing prowess.

Before tasting the next tea, I decided to sample the snack mixture of scalloped-edged onion crackers and small peanut cookies. Though the onion crackers were especially good, they had a way of clouding my palate for the delicate white tea which followed.

The **Silver Needles** tea I found to be light and elusive. The pale liquid seemed to defy description. This, I thought, is the drink of ghosts.

A display case contains samples of various teas and confirms that, while all teas descend from the same *Camellia sinensis* plant, due to factors such as climate, soil, cultivation, and processing, each is unique. Bulk teas range in price from about ten dollars a pound for **Liu An** specialty tea, to a staggering five-hundred-forty-five dollars a pound for the Fong's world-famous **Junshan Yinzhen** green tea (or three dollars per one-serving packet). *Gaiwan*-style and Yixing tea ware, bamboo implements, and various tea sets may also be purchased.

At three o'clock the men of the Bird Club began to disperse. Very mysterious, how each man left with a covered cage. The birds were mostly silent now, though an occasional chirp or rustle could be heard as the men paraded past my table. One elderly man smiled at me mischievously. Soon all that could be heard were the soft, wistful strains of the background "Tea with Flower Fragrance" music.

Afterwards, a walk through Chinatown proper is recommended. Visit the nearby Tai Yick Trading Co. (1400 Powell Street), an amazing shop crowded with porcelain statuary, where gods and goddesses mingle with teapots.

IMPERIAL TEA COURT
1411 Powell Street (at Broadway)
San Francisco, CA 94133

Phone   **(415) 788-6080**

Web   **http://www.imperialtea.com**

Hours   **Every day, 11:00 a.m.–6:30 p.m.**

Transport   * Powell cable car to Powell and Jackson. Walk
              up Powell two blocks to Broadway.
              * 15-Third, 30-Stockton, or 45-Union/Stockton
              Muni bus to Broadway. Walk up Broadway two
              or three blocks to Powell.

Price

Established   July 4, 1993

MENU   TEA TASTING
              KUNG FU STYLE TEAS
              SNACKS

*Tea gives vigor to the body,
contentment to the mind,
and determination of purpose.*

Emperor Shen Nung (circa 2737 B.C.)

JAPANESE TEA GARDEN

The best time to visit the Japanese Tea Garden is in February or March, when the cherry blossom trees are in bloom, transforming it into a pink-and-green wonderland. Stroll along enchanted paths, over bridges and stepping stones. Or perch at the Tea House's wooden counter for a bird's-eye view of the koi fish pond and surrounding lush greenery, which features over a hundred plant varieties (such as gingko, wisteria, and magnolia trees, bamboos, camellias, and azaleas). Leaning on its trellis near the front of the Tea House is a Japanese black pine, which is the oldest plant in the garden. A trickling waterfall nearby adds to the peaceful atmosphere.

Loose-leaf tea (**Green, Jasmine,** and **Oolong**) and a small bowl of salty rice crackers mixed with sweet almond and sesame seed cookies, is served by kimono-clad women in a secluded, outdoor setting. Be forewarned, however, that squirrels (and sometimes birds) will occasionally try to secret away fortune cookies and other treats.

Though the actual Tea House structure (minus its thatched roof of rice straw, which was replaced by shingles) has survived the years, the ceremony of tea itself has become something of a breezy gesture. Here, one can appear wearing casual clothes, children in tow, and order a soft drink without hesitation. Sometimes waitresses seem jaded, over-tired, or both. Nevertheless, the Tea House is one of my favorite sipping and dreaming spots — it has a magic of its own.

Whenever I visit, I always pay my respects to the bronze, meditating Buddha (cast in 1790 and named *Amazarashi-No-Hotoke,* or "The Buddha who sits throughout the sunny and rainy weather without a shelter"). Often there are flowers and coins scattered on his lap, and more than once I have been asked to photograph groups of smiling tourists as they stop on their wanderings to pose before him.

Other highlights include a towering Pagoda, a Lantern of Peace (which was a friendship gift from the children of Japan in 1953), and a *kare sansu,* or "dry landscape" Zen Garden. The gift shop sells souvenir fans, back-scratchers, and toy flutes. (Hidden in shadows just a few steps east of the gift shop is a decorative, boat-shaped *tsukubai*.)

The Japanese Tea Garden, originally called the Japanese Village, was designed by Makoto Hagiwara for the California Midwinter International Exposition of 1894. For thirty years, aside from his gardening duties, Hagiwara also ran the Tea House concession, living with his family (and a stream of Japanese immigrants) in a large house located in the area now known as the Sunken Garden. Unfortunately, the forced relocation of Japanese-Americans during World War II ended the Hagiwaras' long and fruitful association with the Tea Garden. There is a plaque honoring them near the Main Gate.

Who invented the fortune cookie? I wondered one dusky evening at the Tea House. Some believe it was created in 1916 by David Jung, a Los Angeles noodle manufacturer, who was inspired by the way ancient Chinese rebels exchanged their secret messages inside of buns. Others credit Hagiwara and his baker, citing the appearance of the first fortune cookies at the Tea Garden somewhere between 1909 and 1914. Perhaps it is appropriate that its origin remains shrouded in mystery. The fortune cookies are a perennial, offering their pithy (and often surprisingly appropriate) worldly advice to all those who dare peek inside.

A book by Elizabeth McClintock, containing a self-guided tour of the plants of the Tea Garden, is available at the Arboretum bookshop.

JAPANESE TEA GARDEN
Hagiwara Tea Garden Drive (near 9th Avenue and Lincoln)
Golden Gate Park
San Francisco, CA 94118

Phone	**(415) 752-1171, Gift Shop; (415) 752-4227, Entrance Booth**
Hours	*Tea Garden* **open every day, 9:00 a.m.–6:30 p.m., March through September; and 8:30 a.m.–6:00 p.m., October through February** *Tea House* **open every day, 10:00 a.m.–6:00 p.m. (though sometimes closes earlier during winter months due to lack of light)**

Tea House and Moon Bridge, Japanese Tea Garden, circa 1899

Admission	Adults, $3.50; Seniors and Children, $1.25; Under 6, free. (A Tea Garden map is available at ticket booth.) *No credit cards or travelers cheques accepted*
Transport	From Union Square, take the 38-Geary Muni bus to 6th Avenue and Geary. Transfer to 44-O'Shaughnessy (heading south). Bus stops near Tea Garden entrance. When returning downtown, catch bus across the Music Concourse, at the California Academy of Sciences.
Price	🫖 (Admission not included) *Credit cards ($20 minimum) and travelers cheques accepted in teahouse and gift shop only*
Established	1894

MENU
POT OF TEA
COOKIES AND CRACKERS

Tea is nothing other than this:
heat the water, prepare the tea and drink it with propriety.
That is all you need to know.

Sen Rikyu (1522–1591)
Japanese tea master

LUCY'S TEA HOUSE

Resembling a lanai with its bamboo blinds, potted plants, and green-and-peach batik tablecloths, this is a comfortable place, where one might come to read, study, or talk with a friend. Playing cards and games such as Monopoly, Chinese Checkers, and Go! are provided for customers' entertainment. Also on hand are Chinese writing sets and a small library of tea books.

The teahouse, which reflects proprietress Lucy Li's Taiwanese roots, is protected by a "ghost-eater" puppet. Classical music wafts, though sometimes moody ballads, featuring the two-stringed *er-hu*, and pan flutes, can be heard. Near the cash register, figurines of a man and woman relax under a bonsai tree.

The menu is an odd little book, handmade of wood and bound with leather twine. Teas (which are also available in tins) include **Black, Dong-Din, Dragon Well, Green, Oolong,** and **Ti Kuan Yin**. Homemade, tea-based concoctions have evocative names like **Forget-Me-Not, Jealous Lover,** and **Sweet Memory**. Poured hot or iced, these drinks are made with juices, flowers, fruits, herbs, and sometimes milk. Nowhere else will you taste such exotic tea elixirs.

I sampled two iced drinks, **Forest Heaven** and **Forest Rain Drops**. The foaming Forest Heaven blended green Dragon Well tea with orange juice, pineapple juice, and guava. Forest Rain Drops, an Assam tea with milk, was accompanied by a large black straw, for procuring the strange, pearly tapioca "rain drops" at the bottom of the glass.

Tea snacks, such as Rice Cakes and Peanut Butter Toast, complement the sweet teas nicely. The Spicy Dry Tofu consists of tasty tofu cubes which are stacked like small wooden blocks, garnished with cilantro, and speared with a red-frilled toothpick. The hard-boiled Tea Egg, served on a clear Arcoroc plate, had the look of an ancient egg that one might find in a museum.

Tea ice cream, tea floats, and layered cakes, such as Chocolate Mousse, Macadamia Nut, and Tropical Fruit, are also served.

Yixing teapots, as well as a collection of pigs, are on display. I first noticed the pig motif when I happened to glance at the small, flying pig from Indonesia above my table. Then the pig cup, plate, and teapot, all of which were designed by Lucy Li, appeared. Soon I was noticing the pig presence everywhere. My Chinese Zodiac placemat had this to say about the Pig: "Shy but short-tempered. Affectionate and kind to loved ones. You are impulsive and honest. Most compatible with Sheep and Rabbits. Steer clear of other pigs."

Lucy Li, who has traveled far and wide in search of her beloved pigs, was once a schoolteacher in Taiwan who dreamed of having her own tearoom one day. In 1994 she arrived in America, and a year later, after much hard work, opened Lucy's Tea House. One of her first customers, who runs Chef Wang's restaurant around the corner, and, coincidentally, was born under the sign of the Pig, became her husband. ("You collect a live one!" Lucy's mother is reported as saying.) They were married in the year of the Pig, and now have a charming baby, Jeffrey.

"Always keep your wish!" Lucy reminded me, looking about herself with amazement.

LUCY'S TEA HOUSE
180 Castro Street
Mountain View, CA 94041

Phone	(650) 969-6365
Hours	Monday–Thursday, 11:00 a.m.–10:00 p.m. Friday and Saturday, 11:00 a.m.–midnight Closed Sunday
Transport	CalTrain to Mountain View Station. Crossing the parking lot, turn right onto West Evelyn Street. Pass Hope and Blossom Streets. Turn left on Castro. Lucy's Tea House is located in an alleyway between a travel agency and the Town Club bar.

Price

Established   1995

MENU

TEA DRINKS
POT OF TEA
TEA SNACKS
CAKES
TEA ICE CREAMS

I am in no way interested in immortality,
but only in the taste of tea.

Lu T'ung
Chinese poet and tea master,
T'ang dynasty, A.D. 618–907

Little Girl in Chinese Mandarin Costume, by Lewis Carroll, circa 1880

Side by Side
The Golden Tearoom

Don't be fooled by the coffee storefront! Just around the corner, down a pleasant alley dwarfed by skyscrapers, The Golden Tearoom is preparing to open its doors. Here tea master Kathi Wong will perform her unique style of tea ceremonies, and offer tea tastings—hence the name, Side by Side. Once the finishing touches are complete, the water is boiled, and cups are in place, this tearoom promises to be a welcome haven downtown for those in search of peace of mind amidst chaos— and fine tea.

When I visited, I found a happy clutter of boxes, an antique water kettle, and other artifacts. I tried to envision the marble tables with bamboo-like legs, which were specially designed by Ms. Wong to mirror the Chinese coin's symbolism of heaven and earth.

An exquisite flowery aroma caught my attention as tea was served by proprietress Grace Lee on a round orange wicker tray bearing a brown Yixing teapot, a tall, handleless green ceramic cup, and chocolate fortune cookies.

Over three cups of **Pearl Jasmine** tea, we discussed the Chinese tea ceremony's emphasis on communication and enjoyment of the beverage. During the T'ang Dynasty, tea was the drink of scholars and intellectuals, who were known to write and recite poetry created while under its influence. Today, the sharing of tea is a sign of good will and hospitality.

According to Kathi Wong, "the appreciation of tea is manifold: the beneficial effects on the body, the subtle pleasure experienced, and the state of relaxation one feels after drinking it.... "

The menu will probably be eclectic (think dim sum and scones). Along with loose-leaf teas from Mainland China, such as **Iron Goddess Oolong** and **White Silver Tip**, and black and flavored teas, like **Earl Grey** and **Peach** (as well as decaffeinated **Apricot, Ceylon,** and **English Breakfast**), there will be seasonal **Tea Master's Blends**, featuring Ms. Wong's best finds.

The ancient texts of Lu Yü hold a particular interest for Ms. Wong, who studied tea appreciation in Taiwan. Each day, she rises at 3 a.m., then performs a tea ceremony for herself, before going on to roast coffee.

Side by Side is a marriage of worlds: East and West; coffee and tea. Only with an understanding of Yin and Yang — the inherent harmony of opposites — could such a concept ever flourish. At The Golden Tearoom it seems destined to.

SIDE BY SIDE
163 Main Street (between Mission and Howard)
San Francisco, CA 94105

Phone	**(415) 243-8083**
Hours	**to be arranged**
Transport	*** Metro or BART to Embarcadero Station. Main Street is on the south side of Market, between Mission and Howard.**
Price	
Established	**As Chartreuse (when located elsewhere in the Financial District), 1988. Side by Side, 1998**

POT OF TEA
DIM SUM
SCONES

Silently, silently I steal into my chambers.
Deserted.
Deserted and barren is the grand hall.
Waiting.
Waiting for a man who will not return.
Resigned, I go to my tea.

Wang Wei (A.D. 699–761)
Chinese poet of the T'ang Dynasty

URASENKE FOUNDATION

The Urasenke Foundation offers a lovely introduction to *chado*, or the way of tea. A traditional Japanese tea ceremony is presented, following the aesthetic and philosophical form set forth by esteemed tea master, Sen Rikyû, who lived in the sixteenth century. Sen Soshitsu XV, president of the Urasenke Foundation (and a direct descendant of Rikyû), has established these centers worldwide, where, without prior experience, one can be initiated into the way of tea.

Prior to Rikyû's influence, Buddhists priests practiced the ceremonial drinking of tea as an act of devotion. Remembering this, I removed my shoes with what I hoped was Zen-like grace, and gathered with the other guests in the sparsely decorated waiting room. A tiny scroll hung on one wall, and paned windows gave view to greenery outside, which swayed gently in the wind. Despite the many cups of tea I've consumed, on both sides of the Atlantic, here I was aware of my status as beginner. I knew not what to expect, and this manifested itself as both curiosity and mild anxiety. What if I did something wrong?

I felt relieved when Akiko, a woman visiting from Japan, made mention of the fact that she had studied *chanoyu*, or tea ceremony. Of course, mastery of something as paradoxically simple and complex as *chanoyu* can take a lifetime, and two years study is but a drop in the teacup. Still, I would sit next to her, I decided. When she sipped, so would I. No mistakes.

We were led by our co-host and guide, Bettina Vitell, down the hall, past an abstract painting which, for lack of the real thing, serves as a *roji*, or the small garden that surrounds the teahouse. Kakuzo Okakura, in his classic *The Book of Tea*, describes the *roji* as leading to "a world beyond our mundane life."

To her surprise, Akiko had been named the Special Guest; this distinction she seemed to regard as both honor and burden. Shadowing her, I watched her crouch at the opening of the tearoom. She admired the large scroll, the *chabana* (arrangement of tea flowers), the kettle of hot water, then took her place on the *tatami* (straw mat). I followed.

One by one, we all kneeled or sat. Akiko had brought with her a delicate fan for the occasion, which she showed to me, fluttering it before her for lack of a better translation. Like the waiting room, this small, elevated tearoom was also quite bare. White-blinded windows looked west, towards the setting sun.*

Our host, Scott McDougall, appeared. A tall, regal man, he wore a flowing silk kimono and a benevolent expression. Slowly, with great care, he arranged bowl, caddy, whisk, and scoop in their appropriate places near the kettle. Small buckwheat cookies, each branded with the emblem of a gingko leaf, were placed before us. These, and other such treats, are baked in Kyoto, Japan, for the Urasenke tea gatherings.

Our anticipation grew as he whisked the bright green tea powder, or *matcha*. This frothy mixture he presented to Akiko, whose face disappeared behind her bowl as she reverently drank from it.

Apparently our tea would not be served en masse, but rather, bowl by bowl. I was next. While he prepared my tea, I was encouraged to eat my cookie. Its flavor was strange— unlike anything I'd tasted before. Certainly, it was a far cry from the scones I'd had at the St. Francis days before.

Again our host performed his dancelike ritual. I was presented with an attractive green and silver bowl, which reflected the Tea Gathering's summer theme. I drank what appeared to be liquid emeralds. The same process continued for each of the ten guests.

He flicked the *fukusa*, or silk scarf, as though he were a magician. "*Ichigo, ichie*," he remarked. "One occasion, one opportunity." I began to see things in a different way. Perhaps, I thought, it is not so much *what* happens here that's important, but the *way* in which it is done....

After tea, we were shown the bamboo tea scoop (made by the abbot of a Zen temple) and the lacquered tea caddy, which bore the lone image of a firefly and prompted one Argentinean guest to recall the fireflies of her youth. "The very glow of fireflies cleanses the hearts of those who gaze at them. When one is able to view from close up this pure light, a glow radiating indistinct beauty, it hovers with a mysteriousness that suggests a star fallen to earth," Sen Soshitsu has written.

During the ceremony, both Bettina and Scott offered gentle instruction and answered our myriad questions, which served to put us all at ease. The principles of *chanoyu — wa kei sei jaku*, or harmony, respect, purity, and tranquillity — were deftly imparted, leaving us free to fully experience and appreciate the moment.

* Please note that since my visit, the Urasenke Foundation has moved. The tearoom now faces east.

URASENKE FOUNDATION
2143 Powell Street (between Chestnut and Francisco)
San Francisco, CA 94133

Phone	**(415) 433-6553**
Web	**http://www.urasenke.or.jp**
Hours	**Tea Gatherings on the third Friday of each month at 6:00 p.m., by reservation only. Various tea events, workshops, and lectures are presented by the Urasenke Foundation.**
Transport	*** 15-Third or 39-Coit Muni bus to Powell Street * If traveling by car, allow extra time for parking, as it can be difficult in this neighborhood.**
Price	**($15.00 per person, paid in advance)**
Established	**First Urasenke Foundation in Kyoto, Japan, 1940s. San Francisco Foundation, 1981. Worldwide branches may also be found in Australia, Brazil, France, Great Britain, Italy, Mexico, Peru, the United States, and West Germany.**

MENU MATCHA
JAPANESE SWEET

NEW WORLD

A'CUPPA TEA
Gourmet Tea for People on the Run

A'Cuppa carries forth the tea tradition into the 21st century, without sacrificing quality or heart. Set like a jewel in upscale Crocker Galleria near Union Square, this small, contemporary tea bar pours forth a steady stream of black, green, oolong, and white teas. Eye Openers, Nooners, Pick Me Ups, Unwinders, Herbals T-Tonics, X-Treme Elixirs, The Classics, Connoisseur Line, and Special Teas comprise the creative tea list, which promises everything from "a lift to the spirits" to "afternoon Nirvana." Brewed by either the Affinitea Brewing System (a retro-fitted espresso machine designed to quickly extract the tea's "high notes") or by French coffee press (which allows the leaves "to dance around"), these loose-leaf teas are served only in paper cups.

I pointed at random to the large wall menu, selecting **Confucius say "Wake Up!"**, a blend of black tea, cinnamon, and orange. That, and a lemon bar dusted with powdered sugar, provided me with a simple, but satisfying afternoon tea fix. Beverage in hand, I wandered about the gift area that displayed tea-related cards, candles, books, bath and body products, Yixing teapots, bamboo tea strainers, and more.

Other teas and herbal concoctions: **Morning Maté Madness** (almond black tea with roasted maté), **Gypsy Rose Glee** (peppermint, cirtus, rose), **AwwChoo!** (mint, lemon verbena, echinacea, fenugreek), **Body** (black tea, Siberian ginseng, ginger), **The Queen's Cuppa** (English breakfast), and **San Francisco Fog** (black tea, Irish cream, white chocolate, and steamed milk). The Connoisseur Line (brewed traditionally) features teas like **Pu-erh, Black Dragon,** and **Genmaicha**.

Puddles (chocolate cake with mousse in the middle), scones (from apple cinammon to raisin), carrot cake, almond tea cakes, and a Monster New York Cheesecake are just some of the other enticing desserts. International snacks, such as boxed Japanese, Thai, and Greek salads and wrapped sandwiches are also available.

Infused with a love of the leaf by her Japanese mother, proprietress Kim Maloof was raised on green tea. Like others who share a similar passion, she found that the more she investigated the world of tea, the deeper and more mysterious it became. Determined to make fine teas accessible to all, she and partner Brendan Maloof have made a playful, uplifting space—a modern version of Okakura's oasis for weary travelers.

Little touches, like ambient music (though sometimes blues or jazz), Jetson-style lamps, and gerbera daisies suspended from clear glass vases filled with colored water (which reminded me of *chabana*, the tea flowers arranged for the Japanese tea ceremony), strike just the right aesthetic balance. Seating is limited, however—most sip their teas "on the run."

A'CUPPA TEA
Crocker Galleria, Second Level
50 Post Street (between Montgomery and Kearny)
San Francisco, CA 94104

Phone	(415) 986-9958
Hours	Monday–Friday, 7:00 a.m.–6:00 p.m.
	Saturday, 10:00 a.m.–5:00 p.m.
	Closed Sunday
Transport	Muni bus, Metro, F streetcar (historic trolley), or BART to Montgomery Station. (If arriving underground, take the Montgomery/Sutter exit.) Crocker Galleria is a stone's throw away.
Price	
Established	1998

INTERNATIONAL SNACKS
DESSERTS
CUP OF TEA
HOUSE TEA
DAILY TEA TASTINGS
ICED TEA
CHAI

Tea & Company

TEA & COMPANY
World Tea House

Tea & Company is a state-of-the-art teahouse catering to the tea connoisseur. It is also something of a tea nightspot, where patrons can "take out or hang out." Brushed-metal ceiling fans spin to the steady beat of World Music, and the decor — paper lanterns, rattan chairs, and stenciled tea crates — is minimalistic. Of interest are the round, glass-topped tables, which lay open to view letters, travel journal entries, and e-mails such as this one: "Spent the week engaged in an argument with some local who insists he is the direct descendant of Shen Nung, the purported 'Father of Tea'...." The brisk and bustling mood is like that of a train station, perhaps owing to the fact that owners Jill Portman and Gary Shinner themselves travel the globe from Brazil to Nepal in search of best tea leaves, herbs, fruits, and spices.

No surprise, then, that choosing from the more than eighty-five blends, from **Apricot** to **Zhejiang**, can be a daunting task. I opted for **Spiced Mint**, an uplifting trio of peppermint, licorice root, and cloves. Like modern-day alchemists, the knowledgeable Tea & Company "team members" use only triple-filtered water (for purity's sake), and seriously heed such variables as temperature and brewing time. The aromatic result is then delivered to your table, where it is poured from an ergonomic, clear Bodum teapot into a large teacup. "No saucer?" I inquired. "We're not very traditional here," came the swift reply.

In fact, Tea & Company has proclaimed tea "the beverage of the nineties and the new millennium." To support this claim, colorful information cards at The Tea Rack inform novices of tea's many merits — that, for instance, aside from tasting good, it is high in vitamins and antioxidants, and low in caffeine.

Teas, for sipping or buying by bulk, are categorized: Flavored and Scented (such as **California Fields**, which is blended with sunflowers, cactus flowers, and rhubarb essence); Herb and Fruited (such as their organic **Thai Lemongrass**); Black Estate & Black Blend (good old **Irish Breakfast**); Oolong

(**Ti Kuan Yin**, or "Iron Goddess"); Green (**Genmaicha**, with toasted brown rice, from Kyoto); and White (a mild, sweet tea such as **Baiho Cha**).

Though most black teas are invigorating in their own right, those who require an extra-energy boost might want to try the maté and ginseng herbal tonics. A la carte sweets include fig rosemary bars, Earl Grey brownies, shortbread, pies, and some fat-free items. Calistoga and Mexican hot chocolate are also available.

The gift nook offers a variety of teapots, attractive tins, burlap gift bags, and whistling tea kettles. Complimentary tea tastings are held by appointment. On Wednesday evenings there is a tea class.

TEA & COMPANY
2207 Fillmore Street (at Sacramento)
San Francisco, CA 94115

Phone	**(415) 929-TEAS or (888) 832-4884**
Hours	**Monday–Thursday, 7:30 a.m.–10:30 p.m.** **Friday, 7:30 a.m.–11:00 p.m.** **Saturday, 8:00 a.m.–11:00 p.m.** **Sunday, 8:00 a.m.–10:30 p.m.**
Transport	**22-Fillmore Muni bus**
Price	🫖 🫖
Established	**1996**

MENU
DESSERTS
POT OF TEA
POT OF RARE TEA
ICED TEA
CHAI
HERBAL TONIC
TEA TO GO

The first cup moistens my lips and throat;
The second cup breaks my loneliness;
The third cup searches my barren entrail but to find therein some five
thousand volumes of odd ideographs;
The fourth cup raises a slight perspiration—all the wrongs of life pass
out through my pores;
At the fifth cup I am purified;
The sixth cup calls me to the realms of the immortals.
The seventh cup—ah, but I could take no more!
I only feel the breath of the cool wind that raises in my sleeves.
Where is Elysium?
Let me ride on this sweet breeze and waft away thither.

Lu T'ung
poet and tea master of the T'ang Dynasty
Tea-Drinking

TEA TIME
The Tea Lover's Shop

No journey along the teacup trail is complete without a stop at Tea Time. Michael and Molly Klupfell, tea evangelists, attract those who follow the leaf rather than the bean. Through personalized attention, they educate and inspire everyone from students (Stanford University is nearby) to stockbrokers. One cannot help but be impressed by the hundred or so teas they offer — or the way in which the small steamy shop (which was formerly a Christian Science Reading Room) literally brims with tea lore and stories.

Tea Time is "dedicated to the enjoyment of fine quality teas from around the world." There are black teas from India, China, and Sri Lanka. Oolongs. Green teas from China and Japan — and a rare white tea. Scented teas. Blends. Fruit-flavored teas. Herbals, tisanes, and decafs.

The detailed tea list (complete with Pekoe rating) reads like a fine wine list, and includes teas you may never have heard of, such as **Lover's Leap** (a Ceylon from Sri Lanka), **Japanese Cherry** (a green tea with a cherry blossom scent), **Exotic Honey Ginseng,** and **Thé Melange Russe**. There's also a **Blue Eyes** tisane, which is tinted with cornflowers. Molly Klupfell has devised an intricate system involving scoops and brewing times, so that customers can make a perfect cup of tea at home.

Because the weather was sultry, I selected the **Botanical Garden** herbal iced tea, a pleasant mixture of rose hips, lavender, and sage. I also tried the **China Rose Congou** scented black tea, which had a delightfully old-fashioned flavor. Hot teas are served in clear Inspiration tea glasses with colored handles. Chatsfords from England, with their built-in mesh infuser and dripless spout, are the teapot of choice.

Lemon tea bread sufficed. A la carte desserts range from tantalizing tea cookies to poppy seed chocolate swirls, Bundt cakes, and shortbread baby cakes. Scones, in many flavors, are made with cream, rather than buttermilk.

Finger sandwiches revolve at great speed in a six-sided refrigerated case: salmon with cream cheese and caviar...egg with watercress...cucumber with radish....

In the gift area, there are lovely vintage teacups, dating from the 1920s. Some customers, after purchasing theirs, store them in the shop's Teacup Cabinet. Morphy Richards electric kettles, tea cozies (handmade by Aunt Winnie), Lomonosov Russian teaware, Turov's "Peter the Great" 20-cup teapot, and the Bijorcha Thermapot (an ergonomic thermos/teapot) are also sold, as are hard-to-find British teas (like PG Tips, Tetley, Ty·Phoo) and biscuits. Various tea appreciation classes give tea-lovers "the chance to sniff, smell, swirl, and taste."

Teddy bears can be seen taking tea in the window. The Changing of the Bears occurs every season. In springtime, the female bear dons her hat; in winter, her cloak of black velvet.

TEA TIME
542 Ramona Street
Palo Alto, CA 94301

Phone	(650) 32T-CUPS or (877) 32T-CUPS
Web	http://www.tea-time.com
Hours	Monday–Friday, 10:30 a.m.–6:00 p.m. Saturday, 11:00 a.m.–6:00 p.m. Closed Sunday
Transport	CalTrain to Palo Alto Station. Heading east from station, pass through tunnel. Bear right down University Street (not Lytton). Walk three blocks to Ramona Street and turn right.
Price	
Established	1995

TEA SANDWICHES
DESSERTS
POT OF TEA
ICED TEA
MASALA CHAI
TISANE

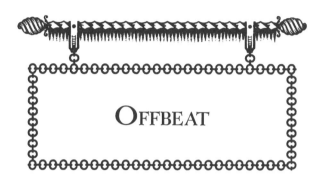

OFFBEAT

CAFÉ ANDREA
SALON DE THÉ

Hidden away in the maze of Stanford Shopping Center, this small, secluded restaurant/wine bar doubles as a tearoom during the bewitching afternoon hours. Its grape-and-mustard color scheme, wood parquet floor, and marble-topped tables create an environment that is at once cozy and refined — reminiscent of an elegant European salon.

When weather permits, outdoor seating is recommended. Take tea in the intimate courtyard, under white umbrellas and lovely jacaranda trees. Here you can watch the occasional lost shopper parading past, perhaps with a Bloomingdale's or Polo Ralph Lauren bag in tow. On the day I visited, I witnessed two well-behaved Schnauzers indulging in heart-shaped dog biscuits.

The courtyard is home, not only to clay pots of flowers, urns of ferns, and topiary ivy, but to *Nature*, a bronze sculpture by Albert Guibara, which depicts a girl holding a bird in her hand, a tortoise, and a lily pad. Elsewhere in the mall, John Pugh's trompe l'oeil village scene is worth seeing.

Café Andrea is named after owners Laszlo and Paulette Fono's daughter. Andrea Fono's colorful, expressive paintings are on exhibit at Café Andrea (and at Bravo Fono and Babbo's, the Fonos' other restaurants, which are located nearby). Strongly influenced by Matisse, she has the distinction of being the official artist for the Centennial of Stanford University.

The tea menu offers Tea for You, Tea for Two, and Sherry or Port with Savories. Tea for You, which, as a woman on my own, I naturally ordered, consisted of homemade scones and tartlets, five gourmet finger sandwiches — cucumber, chicken, tuna, egg, and smoked salmon — and, of course, tea.

The two miniature scones (plain and currant) were baked at the Fonos' bakery, Madame Paulette; raspberry jam and butter in glass bowls proved to be the perfect accompaniment. Mustard, capers, and dill spiced up the finger sandwiches.

Ah, the ubiquitous kiwi! A bite-sized, strawberry-and-kiwi tartlet awaited, as well as a chocolate and lemon tartlet (the latter of which had a discernible zing). These were also homemade.

Tea is poured from an Inox stainless steel teapot (with built-in strainer) into an Arcoroc clear glass teacup. **Black, green,** and **herbal** teas by TWININGS, STASH, and CELESTIAL SEASONINGS are available. Wanting something stronger than **Darjeeling** or **Peppermint**, I tried smoky **Lapsang Souchong** (the flavor of which comes from pine fires).

Though the paper napkin and little basket of sugars containing packets of Equal seemed somewhat out of place, thankfully they did not ruin the dignified effect achieved by the white Cordon Bleu plate.

A la carte pâtisseries include Chocolate Torte (topped with Melba sauce), Tarte au Citron (described as "a tea salon classic"), and Hungarian Apple Strudel. The Frangipane Pear Tart and Tart Praline are served *avec Chantilly,* or with whipped cream.

Brides-to-be and their bridesmaids (and even grooms) may want to partake in a day of indulgences at the mall. Begin at LaBelle Day Spa, which offers a variety of massages, facials, and other body treatments. Then, on to Cornelia Park, which features the whimsical (some say bizarre) MacKenzie-Childs housewares and furniture. Don't forget Victoria's Secret! Next, afternoon tea at Café Andrea, followed by a free jazz concert (during summer months only). Contact Stanford Shopping Center at (650) 617-8585 for details.

Stop the presses! Café Andrea has closed its doors. However, the good news is that Bravo Fono is now serving afternoon tea. In the future, look for an expanded menu, featuring tea styles from around the world (such as British, Chinese, French, and Mediterranean), and teas for children.

CAFÉ ANDREA
c/o Bravo Fono
99 Stanford Shopping Center
180 El Camino Real
Palo Alto, CA 94304

Phone	(650) 322-4664
Hours	Afternoon tea, every day, 3:00 p.m.–5:00 p.m. Restaurant open Monday–Saturday, 11:00 a.m.–10:00 p.m.; Sunday, 11:00 a.m.–6:00 p.m.
Transport	* CalTrain to Palo Alto Station; free Marguerite Shuttle from station to Stanford Shopping Center * From San Francisco by car, take Highway 280 south to Sand Hill Road exit. Head east on Sand Hill Road for a few miles, until you reach the Stanford Shopping Center parking lot.
Price	 *Credit cards accepted; no checks*
Established	1986

 TEA FOR TWO
TEA FOR YOU
SHERRY OR PORT WITH SAVORIES
SCONE OR BRIOCHE WITH BUTTER AND JAM
A LA CARTE PÂTISSERIES
APÉRITIFS
WHITE AND RED WINES
CHAMPAGNES
POT OF TEA

Matrons, who toss the cup, and see
The grounds of fate in grounds of tea.

Alexander Pope
An Essay on Man, 1733

CHAI OF LARKSPUR
Tea Shoppe & Salon

Enveloped by a large rattan chair, gazing out towards the garden, I felt as though I were halfway across the world, perhaps in a time long ago. Proprietress Betty Shelton, an affable woman who laughs easily, describes Chai as "a juxtaposition of the exotic and the serene." This upscale (some say swank) tearoom is utterly unique. Take, for instance, the custom-made Axminster rug with its wild swirls of plumage. Or the tasteful garnish of a chocolate peppermint leaf.

The word "Chai" means tea in Hindi, Mandarin, and Russian. It is not surprising then, that the menu tempts with not only typically British selections like the Chai Classic, Huntsman's High Tea, Sweet Delights, and Cream Tea, but also international tea plates, which are presented in the fashion of a classic English tea: Mediterranean Medley, Middle Eastern Mix, Latin Spice, and French Connection. Young at Heart features, among other treats, a warm chocolate and peanut butter sandwich on brioche.

Chai receives an A+ for artful presentation. The three-tiered tray stood on my table beside the Villeroy and Boch china with a certain poise. The tiny white spoons (meant for the apricot jam, lemon curd, and Devonshire clotted cream), were like the kind a fairy might use. My fanciful, Majolica-style teapot depicted two birds, and its handle resembled a branch of wood.

The Chai Classic consists of gourmet tea sandwiches (cucumber, pear, toasted walnuts, and smoked salmon with seasoned spreads), a warm currant scone, tangy lemon curd squares, spiced apple bread, and shortbread cookies. Though **Classic Earl Grey** tea is suggested, I instead tried the **Republic Chai** (Darjeeling and Assam teas blended with cinnamon, cloves, ginger, and other spices). And, as is the tradition, I added milk.

Many confuse the term "high" tea with "afternoon" tea. The appropriately named Huntsman's High Tea, served with **Kenya** tea, resembles the hearty evening meal which originated with the working-class and is still served in some

Chai of Larkspur

parts of Britain today. It combines a beef and vegetable pasty, crumpets with bacon and sharp cheddar, scone, chocolate meringue cookies, and an apple tartlet.

Other tea choices: **Hibiscus and Herbs, Mango Indica, Rose Petal,** and the caffeine-free **Kids Cuppa**.

The gift corner's finery includes tea cozies (made from antique laces and linens), potpourri, tea strainers, napkin rings, and bookmarks. Dozens of wall-mounted teapots are for sale throughout Chai. In one of the greeting cards I found this quote by Sören Kierkegaard: "Most men pursue pleasure in such breathless haste that they hurry past it." At Chai, of course, this is not the case.

Courtyard seating, under white umbrellas, is available for those who enjoy fragrant roses and birdsong. Out front, where there is some sidewalk seating, colorful pansies grow in window boxes—pansies, because deer ate the hydrangeas.

Chai, which has been voted "Best Tea Salon in the Bay Area" by *San Francisco Focus* magazine, attracts its share of professional women (some juggling briefcases and babies), and even a few discriminating teenagers. Breakfast and lunch are also served. A solo pot of tea provides writers, diarists, etc., an alternative to the café scene. In the guest book you'll find comments like "very civilized," and "reminds me of home."

Aside from harp serenades, psychic tea leaf readings, poetry readings, Teddy Bear Teas, and other events, once a month the tearoom takes on a nightclub atmosphere, when Betty Shelton hosts the popular blues and jazz concerts with The Brown Miget Trio.

CHAI OF LARKSPUR
25 Ward Street
Larkspur, CA 94939

Phone	**(415) 945-7161**
Web	**http://www.chaioflarkspur.com**
Hours	**Sunday, Tuesday, Wednesday, Thursday, 8:00 a.m.–5:30 p.m.**
	Friday and Saturday, 8:00 a.m.–7:30 p.m.

Closed Monday

Transport	* Golden Gate Transit ferry from Pier 0 (behind Ferry Building, at foot of Market Street) to Larkspur Landing; cab to Chai. Call (415) 923-2308 for details. * Golden Gate Transit bus #20 from various Mission Street stops in San Francisco to Magnolia and Ward in Larkspur. Call (415) 923-2000 for details. * From San Francisco by car, take Highway 101 north to Tamalpais/Paradise exit. Bear left onto Tamalpais. Continue toward hills until you reach a three-way stop. Turn right on Magnolia. Right on Ward.

Price

Credit cards and checks accepted

Established   1995

CHAI CLASSIC
HUNTSMAN'S HIGH TEA
SWEET DELIGHTS
CREAM TEA
MEDITERRANEAN MEDLEY
MIDDLE EASTERN MIX
LATIN SPICE
FRENCH CONNECTION
YOUNG AT HEART
TEDDY BEAR TEA (CHRISTMAS)
POT OF TEA

"Have some wine," the March Hare said in an encouraging tone. Alice looked all round the table, but there was nothing on it but tea. "I don't see any wine," she remarked. "There isn't any," said the March Hare.

Lewis Carroll
Alice's Adventures in Wonderland, 1865

CHEZ PANISSE

So much has been written about Chez Panisse and Alice Waters (known as the "Mother of California Cuisine") that I hesitate to add a word. Many have heard of tea diva Helen Gustafson too. That aside, all one really needs to know, before venturing into this wonderland of fine living is that, from the very first sip or taste, reason departs—even the monastery-like decor itself seems to recede—and the sensual power of food and drink takes over.

A neighborhood bistro with a worldwide reputation, Chez Panisse occupies a welcoming wood house with rose-tinted windows and cross-shaped ceiling lights. Named after a character in a 1930s French film trilogy by Marcel Pagnol, its atmosphere is bustling, clublike.

It was an overcast day when I visited Chez Panisse. The clouds sweeping past the stark, tufted silhouette of the Araucaria tree out front promised rain. Inside, classical music was playing—a roving piano concerto. Chefs worked in the kitchen, heads bowed over a mesmerizing array of organic fruits and vegetables.

Between the bewitching hours of lunch and dinner, one can sit at the black marble tables near the café and bar, indulging in fine teas and exquisite desserts. Helen Gustafson, tea buyer (and author of the book *The Agony of the Leaves, The Ecstasy of my Life with Tea*), is always on the prowl for great teas. Since joining Chez Panisse in 1980, she has developed an eccentric list of **Earl Grey, Genmaicha, German Breakfast, Mint, Mugicha, Peach,** and **Yunnan** teas. Glasses of iced Peach tea, infused with the amber essence of peach juice and marigold leaves, and tisanes are also on hand. The teas are served in nubbly black iron teapots accompanied by white Classic Oneida cups and saucers, and the tisanes in clear glass teapots with oh-so-fragile-looking matching cups.

At dinnertime only, the downstairs tea service features specialty teas, such as **Copenhagen Earl Grey, Eshan Pekoe, Heaven-Sent Yin-Yang Pure Jasmine,** and **Margaret's Hope Darjeeling**. After the second seating, the **Ti Quan Yin** and **White Peony** teas are served *kung fu* style, poured from Yixing teapots into cups which are almost as small as thimbles.

In light of the above, I felt fortunate to sample a new **Darjeeling** from the distinguished BLOOMFIELD GARDEN, which had just arrived that day. Refraining from clouding the copper-colored liquid with milk proved wise—on its own, the tea's taste was vibrant and pleasantly astringent.

In-between savoring this rare brew, I nudged bitefuls of Chocolate pavé—a featherlight, flourless cake, decorated with powdered sugar and a drizzle of chocolate sauce—upon my waiting fork. The elevated language of Chez Panisse's menu reads like poetry. Take, for example, the ever-changing dessert selection, which might include Santa Rosa and Elephant Heart plum upside-down cake. Pink Pearl and Gravenstein apple tart with honey cream. Raspberry fool. Black Mission fig and Kadota fig tart with mascarpone and Marsala. Or the rather austere, Haiku-like: Chilled papaya with lime.

Next, for the sake of comparison, I sampled a **Lemon Verbena** tisane. As Helen Gustafson writes in her book: "There is nothing at all mysterious about a tisane...." And yet, the simplicity of the glass teapot, the sight of the whole lemon verbena leaves brewing to a pale, aquatic chartreuse, their heady scent, inspired thoughts of Shen Nung, and alchemists past, and how fortunate I was, to be seated here, suspended in the moment....

CHEZ PANISSE
1517 Shattuck Avenue (between Cedar and Vine)
Berkeley, CA 94709

Phone	(510) 548-5049; (510) 548-5525, reservations only
Web	http://www.chezpanisse.com
Hours	Monday–Thursday, 3:00 p.m.–5:00 p.m. Friday and Saturday, 4:00 p.m.–5:00 p.m. Closed Sunday
Transport	* BART to Downtown Berkeley Station (not North Berkeley), then #43-El Cerrito AC Transit bus north on Shattuck

* From San Francisco by car, take Highway 80 east to University exit. Follow University Avenue about two miles, then turn left on Shattuck.

Price

Credit cards and checks accepted

Established 1971

 A LA CARTE DESSERTS
POT OF TEA
ICED PEACH TEA
TISANE
SPECIALTY TEAS (WITH DINNER ONLY)

*Tea! Thou soft, sober, sage, and venerable liquid,
thou female tongue-running, smile-smoothing, heart-opening,
wink-tipping cordial, to whose glorious insipidity
I owe the happiest moment of my life, let me fall prostrate.*

Colley Cibber
The Lady's Last Stake, 1708

ELIZABETH F. GAMBLE GARDEN CENTER

Take time to literally smell the roses—and other flowers—in this horticultural paradise. Tea is served in the grand, white-columned Main House. Built at the turn-of-the-century in the Colonial/Georgian Revival style, it was once the home of Elizabeth F. Gamble, of Proctor & Gamble fame. In 1981, when Ms. Gamble died, the house was turned over to the City of Palo Alto. Thanks to the grassroots work of the local Garden Club and others, in 1985 the estate was transformed into the Elizabeth F. Gamble Garden Center.

The green front door opened and the guests, many of whom wore sunhats, like myself, were greeted, then seated in either the dining room, living room, or library (where books like the 1935 *Standard Cyclopedia of Horticulture* and the 1889 *Flowers and Flower Lore*, by Reverend Hilderic Friend reside). Oriental carpets, an upright piano, and eggplant-colored drapes set the stage for a tea befitting another era.

"This is much more ladylike than anything I usually do!" one woman remarked as she spread the dainty white embroidered napkin upon her lap.

A small card announced the homemade savories and sweets which adorned the doilied Porcelana plate: Shaved Beef on Roll. Oriental Chicken Salad Sandwich. Mini Toast with Olive Spread. Apricot Cheese Turnover. Lemon Square. Banana Bread. Chocolate Cookie. Strawberry.

Though I enjoyed the innovative Mini Toast with Olive Spread, I found the Apricot Cheese Turnover a bit bewildering for my taste buds. The bill of fare, which changes each month, is prepared by the members and volunteers of this nonprofit community foundation. Many see their task as "a creative outlet," said Dottie Free, who was herself a Home Economics major. As a result of their combined efforts, the afternoon tea experience at the Elizabeth F. Gamble Garden Center rivals that of the best hotels. Teams of white-aproned matrons, one armed with a Portmeirion teapot, shadowed by another carrying a tray of lemon, sugar, and milk, seemed to appear whenever I was downing the last drop of TWININGS teabagged **Earl Grey**. (Iced tea is also available.) The mood was festive. "Cheers!" some guests toasted, and clinked teacups. Before long, the laughter and tea-patter had drowned out the chiming birds outside.

Arrangements of fresh flowers, while attractive, left a curious rain of pollen on the pink tablecloths. Growing out of the fireplace was a large fern. Even the mantle itself overflowed with flowers. The view from the windows was of green...green...green....

A docent is on hand after tea to give a tour of the 2.3-acre wonderland, which is tended by resident horticulturist Donald Ellis. The garden brims with poppies and lavender, cabbages and sunflowers, anemones, wisteria, and forget-me-nots—to name but a few. Highlights include a white gazebo, a few well-dressed scarecrows, and a Victorian grotto. A thought-provoking stanza from The Rubáiyát is inscribed on a sundial: "The moving finger writes; and having writ/Moves on: nor all your piety nor wit/Shall lure it back to cancel half a line/Nor all your tears wash out a word of it."

Cat's Claw grows near the small brick Tea House, where Ms. Gamble entertained her friends, many of whom were affiliated with Stanford Hospital. In fact, she often brought armfuls of her elegant irises as gifts to patients. Today, the many well-tended beds of irises (with names like Peach Face, Soap Opera, and Mystique) serve as reminders of her original passion for that flower.

ELIZABETH F. GAMBLE GARDEN CENTER
1431 Waverley Street
Palo Alto, CA 94301

Phone	**(650) 329-1356**
Hours	**Teas are held from 2:00 p.m.–4:00 p.m., on the third Wednesday of each month, by reservation only. Call or write for details. There are several popular holiday teas during December. The Garden is open daily from dawn to dusk.**
Transport	*** CalTrain to Palo Alto Station; cab to Gamble Garden Center (about ten blocks away).**

* From San Francisco by car, take Highway 280 south to Sand Hill Road exit. Head east on Sand Hill Road for a few miles, passing through Stanford Shopping Center's parking lot. Turn right on El Camino Real, then left on Embarcadero Road (at Town & Country Village). At the second traffic light, turn right on Waverley Street. Park in either of two parking lots.

Price   ($12.50 per person, paid in advance)

Established   Main House and Carriage House, 1902. Garden Center, 1985. Tea has been served in the Main House since 1993.

 AFTERNOON TEA

In teacup times of hood and hoop
Or while the patch was worn.

Alfred, Lord Tennyson (1809–1892)
The Talking Oak

MAD MAGDA'S
Russian Tea Room & Café

Mad Magda's is for the true tea adventurer. Located on the same street as designer dress shops and Powell's Soul Food, this tearoom offers more than tea. "Magic Garden Seating," a sign promises. "Fortunes Told Inside." And, sure enough, on my first visit, I observed a woman shuffling Tarot cards in the window.

The walls are painted like clouds, incense wafts, and it is not uncommon to hear Ethel Waters crooning "Shadows on the Swanee" at Mad Magda's. On an altar looming behind the counter are religious icon candles, Russian dolls, a clock, a samovar, and a military hat, as well as two portraits of owner David Nemoyten's grandmothers. Not surprisingly, tea is served on mismatched china. The tables are small, graced by candles and flowers. Aside from Tarot cards, palms and tea leaves are also read for the curious and/or lovelorn.

No finger sandwiches here. Instead, the so-called "famous" sandwiches have names like Stalin, Cruschev, Catherine the Great, Trotsky, Tolstoy, and Fabergé. Russian tea cakes, chocolate-dipped macaroons, shortbread, and Black Magic cake are among the many desserts, which are baked elsewhere. CAPRICORN black teas include **Ceylon, Darjeeling, Earl Grey, English Breakfast** (regular and decaf), and **Smoked Russian**, as well as scented teas like **Black Currant, Jasmine, Mango,** and **Passion Fruit**. **China Green** tea is also offered. The herbal teas are **Chamomile** and **Peppermint**. **Titania's Tonic** (Smoked Russian tea with honey-steamed milk and a sprinkle of nutmeg) is a popular alternative.

Be sure to venture out to the garden. White lights intertwine with ferns and ivy, and a silver David statue stands between Buddha and a spitting satyr. A birch tree rustles. Recently a stage has been built, probably to accommodate the annual Mysterium (a festival of visual, performance, and mystic arts). It is not hard to imagine pagan rituals of some sort being conducted here—despite the presence of Astroturf.

"A place with a sense of humor is so superior to a place

without one," said Jenna Evans, a wise young woman wearing a turban and fifties-style eyeglasses, who works the counter when she's not giving psychic readings. She explained how people who are "out of the system, but want to do something meaningful with their talent and change the world" are often attracted to Mad Magda's. Apparently this is not just a quirky tearoom, it's a spiritual meeting place.

MAD MAGDA'S
579 Hayes Street (at Laguna)
San Francisco, CA 94102

Phone	(415) 864-7654
Hours	Monday and Tuesday, 8:00 a.m.–9:00 p.m. Wednesday, Thursday, Friday, 8:00 a.m.–midnight Saturday, 9:00 a.m.–midnight Sunday, 9:00 a.m.–7:00 p.m. Tarot, palm, and tea leaves read Monday–Friday, 1:00 p.m.–closing; Saturday and Sunday, 11:00 p.m.–closing
Transport	21-Hayes Muni bus. From downtown, bus stops at Hayes and Laguna. In the other direction, bus stops a block away, at Grove and Laguna.
Price	🫖 🫖 *No credit cards or checks accepted*
Established	1991

SANDWICHES
A LA CARTE DESSERTS
TITANIA'S TONIC
POT OF TEA

O Chamé
Restaurant & Tea Room

At once rustic and classy, O Chamé mirrors the original teahouses of Japan, with its *roji*-like entrance, flower arrangement (a surrealistic tangle of green-tinged callas, pods, and berries on the day I visited), and long-life scroll. One senses the authentic spirit of this place — a trait uncommon in so many of today's trendy new eating and drinking establishments. Etched on walls and ceiling are artist Mayumi Oda's ethereal goddesses, who, as they float above, playing flute and zither, seem to defy both logic and gravity. Other special touches: toadstool-like patio seating, a streetside tea cart, and, on each table, pairs of wooden chopsticks balanced upon pale blue stones.

Using a grill and wood stove, Chef David Varny, who once studied the ritualized *kaiseki* (tea ceremony) style of cooking, creates his own original, Japanese-inspired "meals in a bowl." Intended to be enjoyed with tea, these *suba* (buckwheat) or *udon* (wheat) noodles in a fish-based broth are topped with shrimp and wakame seaweed, shitake mushrooms and daikon sprouts, salmon and bean sprouts, pork tenderloin and mustard greens, aburage (tofu skins) and spinach, smoked trout and wakame seaweed, grilled chicken breast with spinach, or beef with burdock root and carrot. The large steaming bowls arrive at one's table along with *shichimi* (pepper flakes with black sesame seeds and other spices) and, of course, clunky white spoons.

Pre-brewed loose-leaf teas are served in ceramic, handleless mugs. There are a variety of intriguing green teas — **Formosa, Genmaicha, Gunpowder, Hojicha,** and **Jasmine** — and fermented teas such as **Assam, Champagne Oolong, Darjeeling, Keemun, Passion Fruit,** and **Yunnan**. The two iced teas are **Passion Fruit** and tea-bagged **Mugicha**. Beverages, such as Sapporo draft beer, pomegranate spritzer, plum wine, and sake are also offered.

I sipped Genmaicha (nicknamed the "popcorn" tea for its puffed kernels of rice), which was perfectly brewed — not too strong, as is the danger with green teas. Thankfully my strawberry and rhubarb tart (the seasonal selection changes) was accompanied by a fork. Other desserts combine the best of East and West: chocolate tortes, homemade sherry custard, assorted cookies (from chocolate peanut to shortbread), and two types of ice cream—green tea and red bean.

O Chamé is run by David Vardy and his wife, Hiromi. The restaurant's name literally translates as "Eyes of Tea." (The colloquial translation, "Little Precocious One," may relate to their daughter, Lia.) Together they have made a place where the way of tea is as beautiful and unique as it is accessible. Besides, in what other tearoom can one forget the cares of the day, settle back and order a grilled eel appetizer (or, for those on the run, Bento boxed lunches of fish, vegetables, rice)? Only at O Chamé.

O Chamé
1830 Fourth Street (at Hearst)
Berkeley, CA 94710

Phone	**(510) 841-8783**
Hours	**Monday–Thursday, 11:30 a.m.–3:00 p.m. and 5:00 p.m.–9:00 p.m.** **Friday and Saturday, 11:30 a.m.–3:00 p.m. and 5:00 p.m.–9:30 p.m.** **Closed Sunday**
Transport	*** BART to Downtown Berkeley Station (not North Berkeley), then #51-Third/University AC Transit bus to University and Fourth. Turn right on Fourth Street and walk one block to Hearst.** *** From San Francisco by car, take Highway 80 east to University exit. Follow signs to Fourth Street. Be sure to visit nearby shops such as The Gardener (nextdoor), and Elicia's Paper and Restoration Hardware (across the street).**
Price	 *Credit cards accepted; no checks*

Established   1990

APPETIZERS
MEAL IN A BOWL
BENTO BOXED LUNCHES
A LA CARTE DESSERTS
PLUM WINE APÉRITIF
CUP OF TEA

As dusk gave way to the first stars, the women arrived, bowing delightfully....Spicy pickled fruit was passed around on cleverly shaped trays. There then appeared transparent porcelain cups, the size of half an egg, from which the ladies drank a few drops of sugarless tea poured from doll-like kettles.

Pierre Loti
Madame Chrysantheme

SAN FRANCISCO MUSEUM OF MODERN ART
CAFFE MUSEO

For a truly offbeat tea, try MOMA's Caffe Museo, with its birch walls, high ceilings, and black leather-backed chairs which were designed by the museum's architect, Mario Botta. Plan to visit the museum first, which has in its permanent collection of 20th-century art the works of Calder, Klee, Matisse, and Pollack. The ever-changing international crowd makes for excellent people-watching.

Forget quaint. At Caffe Museo, the future is already here: tunic-clad servers rush back and forth bearing wooden trays, and on each table, vials of salt and pepper have replaced common shakers. A beanstalk-like floral arrangement cascades from suspended vases anchored to a concrete slab. It is still possible, however, to glimpse through the windows the lone steeple of St. Patrick's Church (founded 1851) among the patchwork of skyscrapers.

Tea is an à la carte affair. I ordered English Breakfast tea and a hearty strawberry-jam-filled scone; these "house-made" jam fillings change with the seasons. Another option is the rum raisin scone. The black-and-white porcelain, with its dots and zigzags, added a playful touch to my wholesome afternoon tea snack, and, though the wide-spouted teapot proved to be a bit difficult to pour, I did appreciate the options of half-and-half instead of milk, and the packets of brown sugar "in the raw."

TEA & COMPANY (World Tea House) supplies the teas, and Pan-O-Rama , the desserts (from lemon cake, to fresh fruit tarts, to chocolate brownies) and other baked goods. Choose from **Breakfast Americana, California Fields, Earl Gold** (a cut above plain Grey), and **Vanilla Bean** teas. The herbal teas are **Chamomile Citrus Blossom, Ginger Twist,** and **Mo'rockin Mint**. During summer months, sit outside and try their iced California Fields tea, which is served with a stylish black straw and lemon.

Mediterranean-style sandwiches include grilled chicken on focaccia, grilled portobello mushroom on a bun, and applewood-smoked ham and fontina cheese on an Italian

Caffe Museo

San Francisco Museum of Modern Art

"slipper."

Nancy Frumkes DeLong, General Manager of Caffe Museo, is affectionately known as the "in-house tea snob." Before coming to San Francisco, she opened and managed the Guggenheim's tea salon in New York.

In the Museum Store, among the art books and unusual jewelry, you'll discover the latest in chef's aprons and contemporary teapots. Across the street, and worth strolling through, is Yerba Buena Gardens, with its landscaped city block of lawns, plants, fountains—and vintage carousel.

SAN FRANCISCO MUSEUM OF MODERN ART
151 Third Street (between Mission and Howard)
San Francisco, CA 94103

Phone	**(415) 357-4000, SFMOMA; (415) 357-4500, Caffe Museo**
Web	**http://www.sfmoma.org**
Hours	*Museum*, **Monday, Tuesday, Friday, Saturday, Sunday, 11:00 a.m.–6:00 p.m. and Thursday, 11:00 a.m.–9:00 p.m.** *Caffe*, **Monday, Tuesday, Friday, Saturday, Sunday, 10:00 a.m.–6:00 p.m. and Thursday, 10:00 a.m.–9:00 p.m.** **Closed Wednesday and major holidays**
Admission	**Adults, $8.00, Seniors, $5.00, Students, $4.00, Under 12, Free.** *Admission is half-price on Thursdays, 6:00 p.m.–9:00 p.m., and free on the first Tuesday of each month*
Transport	*** Muni bus or F streetcar (historic trolley) to Third and Market. Walk down Third Street a block and a half. * Metro or BART to either Powell or Montgomery Stations. Third Street is between these stations, on the south side of Market. Walk down Third Street a block and a half.**

Price	🫖 🫖 🫖 (Admission not included)
	Credit cards accepted; no checks
Established	1995

MEDITERRANEAN-STYLE SANDWICHES
A LA CARTE DESSERTS
MUFFINS AND SCONES
FRUIT TARTS
POT OF TEA
ICED TEA

They are at the end of the gallery;
Retired to their tea and scandal,
according to their ancient custom.

William Congreve
The Double Dealer, Epistle Dedicatory (1694)

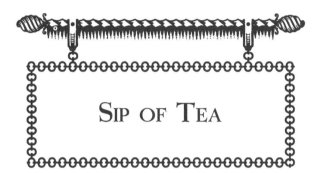

Sip of Tea

ALFRED SCHILLING

Picture ancient Egyptian hieroglyphs marching across the walls, and chocolates shaped like pyramids. World-class chef Alfred Schilling, joined by his team of pastry and chocolate experts, has created an elaborate world within a world: There's a café, restaurant, chocolate factory, and an open kitchen, where the Banana Mousse with its spun chocolate, the Medusa, and the honeycombed Opera Cake are made. Tea is served in the café, and while its wood and purple velvet decor borders on homeliness, the restaurant is rather shrine-like. Outside, there's a patio with a gold-tasseled awning, where you can watch passersby and the tide of cars and trolleys as they hurry along Market and Gough Streets.

Chocolate is something of an obsession for Alfred Schilling. He molds it into masks, seashells, and cherubs (of caramel, white chocolate, Grand Marnier, and curaçao). Wherever one turns, there is chocolate in the forms of colorful butterflies, hearts, or fish. The gift boxes of chocolates are called Tabou. At lunchtime, among other concoctions, a duck stew with chocolate sauce and new potatoes is served. At dinner, in addition to the monkfish and rabbit dishes, the Willy Wonka special features a chocolate starter, chocolate entrée, and chocolate dessert.

Tea appears in a giant cup and saucer: BIGELOW **Earl Grey, English Teatime, Mint Medley,** or **Sweet Dream** (a blend of Chamomile and Hibiscus).

Afterwards, be sure to take an amble around the incredible art and design store nextdoor, Flax.

ALFRED SCHILLING
1695 Market Street (at Valencia)
San Francisco, CA 94103

Phone	**(415) 431-8447**
Hours	*Café*, **Monday–Saturday, 7:00 a.m.–7:00 p.m.** **(and often later, on the nights dinner is served)** *Restaurant*, **Monday–Saturday, 11:30 a.m.–3:00**

p.m. (lunch); Tuesday–Saturday, 5:30 p.m.–10:00
p.m. (dinner)
Closed Sunday

Transport | * Muni bus or F streetcar (historic trolley) to
Market and Valencia
* Metro or BART to Van Ness Station, then walk
about three blocks southwest on Market.

Price

Established | 1996

DESSERTS
CHOCOLATES, TRUFFLES, AND CHERUBS
CUP OF TEA

*My experience...convinced me that tea was better than brandy,
and during the last six months in Africa I took no brandy,
even when sick taking tea instead.*

Theodore Roosevelt (1858–1919)
Letter, 1912

BARNES & NOBLE
Booksellers

The cheerful Irish girls at the counter were singing—"Mary, Mary, quite contrary, How does your garden grow? With silver bells and cockle shells and pretty maids all in a row"—as I pondered the tins of THE REPUBLIC OF TEA: **Blackberry Sage, British Breakfast, Cardamom Cinnamon, Cinnamon Plum, Earl Greyer, Ginger Peach, Mango Ceylon** (decaf), and **Tea of Inquiry.** Overhead, a colorful mural of a European café scene depicted a virtual writers' heaven, in which Fitzgerald, Parker, Faulkner, Steinbeck, Eliot, Singer, Kafka, Neruda, Hughes, Tagore, and Hurston appeared deep in conversation. Only Faulkner appeared to be drinking tea, however; perhaps chamomile?

In this surprisingly homey corner of Barnes & Noble bookstore, the billiards-green tables are flanked by green upholstered chairs. There is some window seating. You might find a businessperson reading a newspaper, a flock of tourists who have strayed from Fisherman's Wharf proper, or even a dutiful child doing homework. In the distance, book-lovers dreamily ascend and descend the escalator that bridges fiction and nonfiction.

Hot tea is served in a hefty glass mug, and the sweets on an Arcoroc plate. Choose from madeleines, fudge brownies, lemon bars, scones (orange currant or raspberry), luscious carrot and German chocolate cakes, and other sweets, as well as sensible-looking sandwiches (wrapped in cellophane), vegetarian quiche (with soy "bacon"), and hot clam chowder with sourdough bread.

BARNES & NOBLE
2550 Taylor Street (at Bay)
San Francisco, CA 94133

Phone	**(415) 292-6762**
Web	**http://www.barnesandnoble.com**

Hours	Every day, 9:00 a.m.–11:00 p.m.
Transport	* 42-Muni bus to Taylor and Bay * Powell-Mason cable car to Taylor and Bay
Price	
Established	Wheaton, Illinois, 1873. San Francisco, 1995

SANDWICHES
CLAM CHOWDER
DESSERTS
SCONES
CUP OF TEA
ICED TEA

Tea, though ridiculed by those who are naturally coarse in their nervous sensibilities...will always be the favored beverage of the intellectual.

Thomas DeQuincey
Confessions of an English Opium Eater, 1822

BORDERS
Books · Music · Café

In the name of books, tea-people and coffee-people unite. Take tea at Café Espresso on the second floor, by the large, arched windows overlooking Union Square, or sit elbow-to-elbow at the counter. Strategically placed near the cooking section, the Café is a vision of bricks, tiles, and wood, with playful accents of purple and orange. Modern lamps hang overhead, held aloft by a series of cords, weights, and pulleys. There are over 120,000 books at Borders (not to mention their music, video, and new media titles) and a good many of them make their way to the Café. In fact, when local or touring musicians are not giving live performances in the corner, the busy atmosphere is much like that of a library.

Teas are all by THE REPUBLIC OF TEA. The extensive list features a spectrum of black, green, and herbal teas, among them **British Breakfast, Desert Sage, Ginseng Peppermint,** the rare **Sky Between the Branches, Tea of Inquiry,** and **Vanilla Almond**. A few decaffeinated teas are also offered. Due to the absence of teapots, round, stringless tea bags are instead submerged into white Homer Laughlin mugs with matching saucers. Borders' own brand of **Chai**, described as a "tea latté," is a spicy ginger and honey grog, served hot or cold.

The line moves quickly, leaving one little time to decide between savories, grilled panini sandwiches, pasta salads, "personal" pizzas, and soups—not to mention the scones (apple cinnamon, strawberry, currant, olallieberry) and other sweets, such as the Raspberry Linzer Torte or the Apple Raisin Spice Cake.

BORDERS
400 Post Street (at Powell)
San Francisco, CA 94102

Phone   **(415) 399-1633**

Web   **http://www.borders.com**

Hours	Monday–Thursday, 9:00 a.m.–10:30 p.m. Friday and Saturday, 9:00 a.m.–11:30 p.m. Sunday, 9:00 a.m.–8:30 p.m.
Transport	From Market and Powell Streets, walk up Powell four blocks to Post.
Price	
Established	Ann Arbor, Michigan, 1971. San Francisco, 1994

SAVORIES
SANDWICHES
DESSERTS
SCONES
CUP OF TEA
CHAI

We haven't had any tea for a week...
The bottom is out of the Universe.

Rudyard Kipling (1865–1936)
Natural Theology

Café Hana

The black tables bearing potted white cyclamen are shaped like boomerangs, and the fern, bamboo, and ivy form a miniature haunted forest in this informal Japan Center conservatory setting. Around the corner, at the Isobune restaurant, can be seen colorful floating trays of sushi in a swirling moat, the water of which separates chefs from patrons. Elsewhere, the starkly elegant plumes of goodwill and friendship flowers command one's attention at the Ikenobo Ikebana Society of America.

Desserts range from Mango Crème Brulée or Chocolate Raspberry Marquise to the wallflowerish, plain lavender circle of the Raspberry Cheesecake. There are also tarts, eclairs, and scones. Not to mention outrageous truffles. *And* ice cream, by cup or cone, in the exquisite flavor of green tea and vanilla. Azuki, mochi, whipped cream, and a maraschino cherry top the dish called Mochi Ice Cream. The Uji Mochi Freeze is a green tea slush with mini mochis and a twist of lemon. The Geisha Float is another variation—as, yet again, is the Geisha Float Ichiban.

SHIRAKIKU brand **Japanese green** tea and **Genmaicha** are served by the cup or pot. Other tea choices include STASH **Earl Grey** (regular and decaf), **English Breakfast, a sampling of spiced teas, Chamomile, Peppermint**; as well as a few fruity LIPTON teas, like **Blackberry** and **Raspberry**. There's something for everyone—whether it's tea, beer, chocolates, or a green tea ice cream cone.

Café Hana
Kintetsu Building, Japan Center
1737 Post Street, Suite 2 (between Webster and Buchanan)
San Francisco, CA 94115

Phone	(415) 567-9133
Hours	Monday, Tuesday, Wednesday, Thursday, 8:00 a.m.–9:00 p.m. Friday and Saturday, 8:00 a.m.–10:30 p.m.

Sunday, 8:00 a.m.–9:00 p.m.

Transport   From Union Square, take the westbound 38-Geary Muni bus at Geary and Stockton to Geary and Webster, or the westbound 2-Clement, 3-Jackson, or 4-Sutter bus at Sutter and Stockton to Sutter and Webster. From other points, take the 22-Fillmore to Geary and Fillmore. Be sure to visit nearby Kinokuniya Bookstore.

Price

Established   1994

DESSERTS
MOCHI DISHES AND GEISHA FLOATS
TRUFFLES
BEER (DOMESTIC AND IMPORTED)
POT OF TEA
CUP OF TEA
ICED TEA

Do Katydids drink tea?

Oliver Wendell Holmes (1809–1894)
To an Insect

CALIFORNIA PALACE OF THE LEGION OF HONOR
LEGION OF HONOR CAFÉ

High in the mists above Lincoln Park, overlooking the Pacific Ocean, this neoclassical building casts a spell of enchantment. Visitors to the museum are met by two horn-playing angels, and Rodin's *The Thinker*, who appears to be in need not only of new insights, but of a good cup of tea.

Wind your way through 4,000 years of art — past the *English Looking Glass, Sedan Chair*, and the *Egyptian Torso of a God* — to the spacious Legion of Honor Café, where luscious, dignified cakes (by Sweet Things) take on the importance of relics. There are Bundt cakes, Orange Angel Food, and Black Magic cakes. Round, individually-sized cheesecakes (sour cream or chocolate), by Mendocino's Cheesecake Lady. Shortbread, cookies, brownies, apricot bars, and even house-baked apples add to the temptations. (The homemade black currant and ginger scones tend to disappear by afternoon.) A variety of sandwiches — such as honey-roasted eggplant, goat cheese, tomatoes, and sweet basil on focaccia — soups, salads, and hot daily specials, are also served.

Take tea in dainty Mikasa teacups and saucers. The TWININGS tea bag selection is small but adequate: **Darjeeling, Earl Grey, English Breakfast, Chamomile,** and **Mint**. (The **Earl Grey** and **English Breakfast** are also available decaf.)

Though the Café window, Bruce Beasley's *Knight's Gambit II* can be viewed. On the patio, amongst the olive trees, you'll find other examples of modern art: Arnaldo Pomodoro's *Sfera #2* and Joel Shapiro's *Untitled*, which, in my opinion, resembles a teepee on the verge of collapse.

For those with more traditional tastes, be sure to see the Constance and Henry Bowles Porcelain Gallery, which is home to 18th- and 19th-century teaware from around the globe. Also of interest: *The Traveling Beverage Service*, and, elsewhere in the museum, the *Fabergé Tea Service and Table*, and two lovely silver gilt samovars.

Call for details about weekend Harvest Teas, at which tea-drinkers are serenaded on the Legion's Skinner organ.

CALIFORNIA PALACE OF THE LEGION OF HONOR
390 Legion of Honor Drive (near 34th Avenue & Clement Street)
Lincoln Park
San Francisco, CA 94121

Phone	(415) 750-3600, Museum; (415) 863-3330, 24-Hour Hot Line; (415) 221-2233, Café
Web	http://www.thinker.org
Hours	*Museum*, Tuesday–Sunday, 9:30 a.m.–5:00 p.m. *Café*, Tuesday–Sunday, 9:30 a.m.–4:00 p.m. Closed Monday and major holidays
Admission	Adults, $7.00; Seniors, $5.00; Youth (12–17), $4.00; Under 12, Free. *Free admission on the second Wednesday of each month*
Transport	38-Geary Muni bus to 33rd Avenue and Geary. If you're feeling extremely energetic, walk up Geary to 34th, turn right, and head northwest along Legion of Honor Drive through Lincoln Park (watching out for golf balls) to the very top of the hill. Otherwise, transfer to the 18-46th Avenue Muni bus.
Price	🍵/ 🍵 (Admission not included)
Established	Museum, 1924. Café, 1995. The Legion was a gift from Alma Spreckels (wife of the sugar magnate) to the people of San Francisco, honoring the Californians who died in World War I.

SANDWICHES
DESSERTS
SCONES
HOUSE-BAKED APPLES
CUP OF TEA

CINDERELLA

Located near Golden Gate Park, on foggy Balboa Street, the Cinderella bakery/restaurant has been quietly serving borscht, piroshki, and pastries to a mostly Eastern European clientele since 1966.

Tea is an informal affair, served in dowdy cafeteria-style cups. LIPTON **black** tea, and BIGELOW **herbal** teas (**Cranberry Apple, Orange and Spice, Mint Medley**) are accompanied by slices of lemon, though, in the case of the "brisk" tea, milk may be requested. Butter cookies, cakes, meringues, cottage cheese pies, and poppy seed rolls are among the bakery's many treats.

White lace curtains and a timeless atmosphere add a storybook feel to the Cinderella. On display is a golden samovar, like the kind once used to brew tea during the long camel treks between China and Russia. The colorful posters of Moscow, white-haired Russian doll, and gusli (a musical instrument played during the telling of fairy tales) set the mood for a charming, if humble, little tea.

CINDERELLA
436 Balboa Street (at 6th Avenue)
San Francisco, CA 94118

Phone | **(415) 751-9690**

Hours | **Tuesday–Saturday, 9:00 a.m.–9:00 p.m.**
Sunday, 9:00 a.m.–7:00 p.m.
Closed Monday

Transport | **31-Balboa Muni bus**

Price |

Established | **1966**

PIROSHKI AND BORSCHT
DESSERTS
CUP OF TEA

Dancers Around the Doré Vase, de Young Museum, circa 1926

DE YOUNG MUSEUM
CAFÉ DE YOUNG

The de Young, which dates back to the Midwinter International Exposition of 1894, has the distinction of being San Francisco's oldest public museum. Among its many treasures, you'll find Dirk van Erp's *Kettle, Stand, and Burner*, Cyprian Wilcox's *Sugar Tongs*, and *Elements from a Tea Set*. Two separate rooms recreate with eerie precision George III's dining room (which is arranged for an afternoon dinner party) and the gloomy Smith parlor (complete with fireplace, drapes, and teacups and saucers on the mahogany table). In the adjacent Asian Art Museum, be on the lookout for the jeweled jade cup with two handles, and the fascinating window display of Japanese tea ceremony utensils — from kettle to whisk. I came away with a sense of tea's pervasive influence, from country to country, from past to present.

Never underestimate the reviving power of TWININGS **Orange Pekoe** and a peanut sunflower cookie — especially if taken in the enchanted garden courtyard, with its pink camellias and Victorian-inspired latticework, where cherub statues perpetually cavort around a stately pool of stones and grasses. This is the kind of spot where one might huddle with a friend beneath one of the large white umbrellas, or simply lean back and watch the changing sky overhead. The cafeteria itself, located on the other side of the French doors, is clean and civilized, displaying on its cream-colored walls a few gilt-framed oil paintings.

Other tea bag choices (served in Arcoroc mugs): **English Breakfast, Chamomile,** and **Mint**. Museum-goers may also be fortified by homemade salads, soups, and sandwiches such as Black Forest Ham, Swiss Cheese and Sprouts, or Peanut Butter and Jelly. Desserts (by Sweet Things) feature a variety of tarts, Bundt and layer cakes, cookies, and Fruit Nut Hermits.

Tucked away in the center of the de Young is Gallery One, a special exhibition for children, complete with a computer station, displays, and reading, writing, and drawing areas. The Asian Art Museum (which is scheduled to move to the old Main Library building by the end of 2,000) houses the largest collection of Asian art in the western world.

DE YOUNG MUSEUM
75 Tea Garden Drive (near 10th Avenue and Fulton)
Golden Gate Park
San Francisco, CA 94118

Phone	(415) 750-3600, Museum; (415) 863-3330, 24-Hour Hot Line; (415) 752-2536, Café
Web	http://www.thinker.org
Hours	*Museum*, Wednesday–Sunday, 9:30 a.m.–5:00 p.m. *Café*, Wednesday–Sunday, 9:30 a.m.–4:00 p.m. (On the first Wednesday of each month, the museum stays open until 8:45 p.m., and the Café is open during the evening, 6:00 p.m.–8:00 p.m.) Closed Monday and Tuesday, and major holidays
Admission	Adults, $7.00; Seniors; $5.00; Youth (12–17), $4.00; Under 12, Free. *Free admission on the first Wednesday of each month*
Transport	From Union Square, take the 38-Geary Muni bus to 6th Avenue and Geary. Transfer to 44-O'Shaughnessy (heading south). Bus stops near museum entrance. Returning downtown, catch bus across the Music Concourse, at the California Academy of Sciences.
Price	🫖 🍵 (Admission not included)
Established	Museum, 1894

SANDWICHES
DESSERTS
FRUIT NUT HERMIT
CUP OF TEA

DRAEGER'S MARKET PLACE

Be sure to pay a visit to Draeger's new epicurean wonderland. On the first floor, you'll encounter dazzling displays of flowers and produce, a bakery, deli, and aisle after aisle of a state-of-the-art grocery store. It seems that every item ever recorded on a gourmet's shopping list—from sushi to candied violets—is here. Upstairs, cookbooks and winged Versace teacups serve to inspire even the kitchen-challenged.

The site for tea is the streamlined coffee bar, with its black metal tables and chairs, which is situated just around the corner from the bakery's sumptuous array of freshly-baked cream puffs, eclairs, shortbread cookies, tartlets, and lemon squares. And there's more: buttermilk scones with California raisins, fondant-glazed napoleons, and plump, chocolate-dipped strawberries. The Midnight Moon cake, which resembles a slouch hat of chocolate suede, always draws many stares.

At the insistence of Culinary Director Bill Wallace, teapots are first scalded, then the loose tea is wrapped, potpourri-style, in untreated paper. DRAEGER'S own brand and HARNEY & SONS black and flavored teas include **Black Currant, Earl Grey, English Breakfast, Jasmine, Mango,** and **Orange Pekoe; Egyptian Chamomile, Raspberry,** and **Rose Hip** tisanes, and traditional Chinese teas such as **Formosa Oolong, Keemun,** and **Lapsang Souchong**. Decaffeinated teas are also available.

At the Draeger's in Menlo Park (which Gustave Draeger founded back in 1955, in the days of Blue Chip stamps, and when two pounds of peaches cost only a quarter), you can watch the pastry chefs perform their magic in an open kitchen, then sample tea and cakes in the Top of the Market Bistro overlooking the atrium.

DRAEGER'S MARKET PLACE
222 E. Fourth Avenue (at B Street)
San Mateo, CA 94401

Gustave Draeger and the Original San Francisco Store, 1931

other Bay Area locations:
1010 University Drive, Menlo Park, CA 94025
(650) 688-0677
342 First Street, Los Altos, CA 94022
(650) 948-4425

Phone	(650) 685-3700, Market Place; (650) 685-3785, Coffee Bar
Hours	Every day, 7:00 a.m.–10:00 p.m.
Transport	* CalTrain to San Mateo Station. Turn left and walk briefly along Main Street. Turn right on Third, then left on B Street. * From San Francisco by car, take Highway 280 south to the Highway 92/East exit. Head north on El Camino Real. Turn right on 4th Street. Look for a large, clay-colored building on your right.
Price	
Established	1925. The original San Francisco Draeger's (which has since closed), was followed by family-run markets in Menlo Park (1955), Los Altos (1986), and San Mateo (1997)

DESSERTS
SCONES
CHOCOLATE-DIPPED STRAWBERRIES (SEASONAL)
POT OF TEA
TRADITIONAL AND FLAVORED ICED TEAS

*There is a great deal of poetry and fine
sentiment in a chest of tea.*

Ralph Waldo Emerson (1803–1882)
Letters and Social Aims

GRACE CATHEDRAL
GIFT SHOP

The first Grace Cathedral, known as Grace Chapel, was built at another site in 1849, the year of the Gold Rush; another incarnation was lost to fire in the 1906 earthquake. Today's spectacular French Gothic cathedral atop Nob Hill attracts pilgrims and sightseers alike, many of whom come to walk the winding paths of its indoor and outdoor labyrinths.

The labyrinth is a tool for spiritual growth. It is, in the words of the Reverend Dr. Lauren Artress, "...an archetype, a divine imprint, found in all religious traditions in various forms around the world." The two labyrinths at Grace Cathedral — one, of wool tapestry, near the Great Font; the other, of stone terrazzo, near the Interfaith Garden — are based on the design of the labyrinth at Chartres, France, which dates back to 1220. The three stages of the walking meditation are Purgation, Illumination, and Union.

The Gift Shop, with its oriental carpets and resident harmonium, is located at crypt level. Over a paper cup of TAZO (**Calm, Spice, Passion, Wild Sweet Orange**) or LIPTON (**black** or **herbal**), one can sit outside (weather permitting) and reflect upon the labyrinth experience, or simply browse the hodgepodge of books, CDs, T-shirts, gargoyles, rosaries, icons, and even a few silver chalices. Gregorian chants often fill the shop, adding to its peaceful mood. Come here for more than tea — a cup of Grace.

GRACE CATHEDRAL
1011 Taylor Street (at California), on Nob Hill
San Francisco, CA 94108

Phone	**Cathedral, (415) 749-6300; Gift Shop, (415) 749-6304**
Web	**http://www.gracecathedral.org**
Hours	*Cathedral*, **Sunday–Friday, 7:00 a.m.–6:00 p.m. Sunday, 8:00 a.m.–6:00 p.m. (hours sometimes**

change)
Please note that the outdoor labyrinth is open at
all times, while the indoor labyrinth is only
accessible during Cathedral hours.
Gift Shop, Monday–Saturday, 10:00 a.m.–5:00
p.m.
Sunday, 9:30 a.m.–11:00 a.m. and 12:30 p.m.–3:30
p.m.

Transport
* 1-California Muni bus. From downtown, bus
stops by Huntington Park, at Sacramento and
Sproule. In other direction, bus stops a block
away, at Clay and Taylor.
* California cable car to California and Taylor
* Powell cable car to Powell and California.
Walk up California Street two blocks to Taylor.

Price

Established
Grace Chapel, 1849. Grace Cathedral on Nob
Hill, 1964

SHORTBREAD
CUP OF TEA

O Tea! O leaves torn from the sacred bough!
O stalk, gift born of the great gods!
What joyful region bored thee? In what part of the sky
Is the fostering earth swollen with your health,
bringing increase.

Pierre Daniel Huet
Tea Elegy (circa 1709)

GREENS
Restaurant

During tea-time, sippers are welcome to pull up a chair in the lovely dining room, with its redwood sculpture and spectacular waterfront view (don't be surprised by the sound of foghorns). Enjoy an informal cup of TAZO tea—**Awake, Calm,** a very perfumey **Earl Grey, Passion, Refresh, Spice, Wild Sweet Orange, Zen**—and sample the tasty Greens To Go menu of fresh fruit cobblers, scones, tarts, and other treats (baked on site, and elsewhere), creative sandwiches, salads, soups, and even a black bean chili.

Night owls and romantics flock to Greens for late evening desserts, such as Ricotta Cheesecake with Pistachio Shortbread Crust and Blackberry Fig Compote, or Ginger Crunch Cake with Mascarpone Cream and Poached Blueberries. COFFEE TEA & SPICE and WINDWARD TRADING COMPANY provide an array of loose-leaf teas, which are served in pots: **Apricot, Black Currant, Cinnamon Orange Spice, Darjeeling, Earl Grey** (regular and decaf), **English Breakfast, Jasmine; Chamomile, Hibiscus, Peppermint; Genmai Cha** and **Taiwan Green Sencha. Fresh Mint Tea** (from Green Gulch Farm) is also served. **Mango Indica** and **Peppermint** are the iced teas. The Chai is made with either Strauss organic milk or soy milk. (Note: Look for an influx of organic teas in the future, as Greens revamps its tea list.)

Fort Mason, which for two-hundred years was home to the military, is now a thriving cultural center occupied by unique galleries, museums, theatres, and a variety of nonprofits. Greens, which is owned by the San Francisco Zen Center (who also own Green Gulch Farm and Tassajara Mountain Retreat), is nationally recognized for its vegetarian cuisine.

GREENS
Fort Mason
Building A
San Francisco, CA 94123

Phone	(415) 771-6222
Hours	*Greens To Go,* afternoon tea snacks, Monday–Friday, 2:00 p.m.–4:45 p.m. and Saturday, 2:30 p.m.–4:30 p.m. *Late Evening Desserts,* Monday–Saturday, 9:30 a.m.–11:00 p.m. Inquire for complete Greens To Go, breakfast, brunch, lunch, and dinner hours.
Transport	* 28-19th Avenue Muni bus to Fort Mason. The 22-Fillmore, 30-Stockton, and 43-Masonic go within walking distance of Fort Mason. * Free on-site parking
Price	
Established	Fort Mason Center, 1977. Greens, 1979. Greens To Go/Food to Take Out, 1992

FRESH FRUIT COBBLERS, SCONES, AND TARTS
SANDWICHES
CUP OF TEA

LATE EVENING DESSERTS
POT OF TEA

"Take some more tea," the March Hare said to Alice very earnestly. *"I've had nothing yet,"* Alice replied in an offended tone, *"so I can't take more."*

Lewis Carroll (1832-1898)
Alice's Adventures in Wonderland, 1865

I LOVE CHOCOLATE

Proprietress Mary Brinkmann, who was raised among bakers, studied the art of pastry-making at The Ritz in Paris. "I really do love chocolate," she insists. And one tends to believe her, for she offers a dozen or so varieties of chocolate cake alone, from the namesake cake (semi-sweet and white chocolate mousse with a chocolate ganache icing) to the matronly cake of German chocolate. All chocolate is made by the local Guittard Chocolate Company.

Pastries abound in this small bakery/café. There are scones (apricot, lemon poppy seed, and olallieberry, to name but a few). Tarts and eclairs. Cream puffs and chocolate-dipped shortbread cookies...

Tea is served, not in teapots, but in tall glass mugs. Choose from TWININGS **Ceylon Supreme, China Black, Darjeeling, Earl Grey, English Breakfast, Irish Breakfast, Jasmine,** and **Prince of Wales**. LINDSAY'S fruit-flavored and herbal teas spice up the list: **Apple Cinnamon Orange Fruit, Blue Eyes, Honey Ginseng, Lemon Hibiscus, Mango Banana Pineapple Fruit, Peppermint Chamomile,** and **Very Very Strawberry Fruit**.

Seat yourself inside, in the loft (reachable by a few stairs), or outside, at a sidewalk table. The intimate loft is decorated by a poster of Audrey Hepburn in *Breakfast at Tiffany's*, charming old-time San Francisco photographs, and a large gold mirror. Leaf by leaf, a philodendron creeps its way along the pastel sky- and peach-colored walls, perhaps aiming for the sweet-smelling kitchen.

I LOVE CHOCOLATE
397 Arguello Boulevard (between Clement and Euclid)
San Francisco, CA 94118

Phone	**(415) 750-9460**
Hours	**Every day, 6:30 a.m.–6:00 p.m.**
Transport	**2-Clement, 33-Stanyan, or 38-Geary Muni bus**

Price 🫖

Established 1994

 DESSERTS
CHOCOLATE CAKE
SCONES
CUP OF TEA

If you are cold,
tea will warm you;
if you are too heated, it will cool you;
if you are depressed, it will cheer you;
if you are excited, it will calm you.

W. E. Gladstone (1809–1898)

JUST DESSERTS

Local legend goes like this: Long ago, in the early '70s, Elliot Hoffman made a birthday cheesecake for his wife, Gail Horvath. The serendipitous cheesecake, which was based on a recipe created by a friend's grandmother, proved to be such a success that it soon went public in their neighborhood café. To meet the demand for their dessert, the couple found themselves baking cheesecake after cheesecake in their Noe Valley home. Then, having raised $500 by selling their VW bug, they opened the first bakery on Church Street—and the rest, as they say, is history.

While each of the award-winning Just Desserts serves the same consistently scrumptious fare, the decor and ambience do vary somewhat, depending on location. At Church Street, for instance, the staff share an eclectic appreciation of music—tastes range from rap to unknown bands to the haunting melodies of Dead Can Dance; one never knows what might blare forth next. At the Embarcadero, the mood is more subdued, perhaps due to its shopper clientele and the presence of sleek, space-age furniture. Tassajara Bread Bakery in Cole Valley was run by Zen monks before it joined forces with Just Desserts in 1992; on rainy days, one can still sense a lingering meditative atmosphere. (At this location only, Irish Soda Muffins are served with dollops of raspberry or apricot preserves and a variation of clotted cream.)

Teas (in bags) are by TAZO, a company known for its appreciation of the esoteric (and whose name, in the Romany Gypsy language, means *river of life*): **Awake** and **Earl Grey** black teas, **Zen** green tea, and **Calm, Refresh, Passion, Spice,** and **Wild Sweet Orange** herbal infusions. Tazo's bottled microbrewed tea drinks come in flavors such as **Lemon Ginger, Passion Potion, Tazoberry,** and **Wild Sweet Orange**.

"Life is uncertain...eat dessert first," read Just Desserts T-shirts. In keeping with this motto, choose from a variety of freshly baked treats, including cakes (Carrot, Triple Lemon, and Poppyseed), tarts, scones (buttermilk raisin, strawberry, herb and cheese), "lite" Angel Food Cake, sinful Chocolate Cloud Chiffon (an amaretto-laced mousse), and three different types of cheesecakes: Fruit Topped, Chocolate Chunk, and, of course, The Original.

JUST DESSERTS
San Francisco
248 Church Street (at Market Street) 94114
(415) 626-5774

3 Embarcadero Center, Lobby Level 94111
(415) 421-1609

836 Irving Street (at 10th Avenue) 94122
(415) 681-1277

3735 Buchanan (at Marina Boulevard) 94123
(415) 922-8675

1000 Cole Street (at Parnassus Avenue) 94117
(415) 664-8947

Plaza Foods, 1750 Fulton (at Masonic) 94117
(415) 441-2207

Berkeley
1823 Solano (at Colusa Avenue) 94706
(510) 527-7344

2925 College Avenue (at Ashby Street) 94705
(510) 841-1600

Oakland
4001B Piedmont (at 40th Street) 94611
(510) 601-7780

Palo Alto
535 Bryant Street (at University Avenue) 94404
(650) 326-9992

Hours	Call the location in question for details.
Transport	Call Muni at (415) 673-MUNI; BART at (510) 464-6000; or CalTrain at (800) 660-4287.

Price

Established   1974

DESSERTS
SCONES
LEMON TART
IRISH SODA MUFFIN
MICROBREWED TEA DRINKS
CUP OF TEA
ICED TEA

A hardened and shameless tea-drinker, who has for twenty years diluted his meals with only the infusion of this fascinating plant; whose kettle has scarcely time to cool; who with tea amuses the evening, with tea solaces the midnight, and with tea welcomes the morning.

Dr. Samuel Johnson (1709–1784)
author of the first English dictionary, referring to his tea habit

KOWLOON
Vegetarian Restaurant

Just down the street from Ten Ren Tea, across from the ancient lantern of Li Po Cocktails, stands Kowloon. This modest Chinatown restaurant is watched over by a statue of the goddess Kuan Yin. While patrons flick chopsticks, she calmly meditates in a shrine filled with fruit offerings and burning wands of incense.

Sip TEN REN loose-leaf **Jasmine** or **Oolong** tea, which is poured from quaint blue-and-white teapots into matching handleless cups. In the glass case you'll find dim sum (which translates as "heart's delight") and sweets such as Moon Cakes (made from red bean paste, mixed nuts, or lotus bean paste). Winter Melon Cake, Flower Cake, Taro Root Cake, and Butterfly Cookies also beckon. Ice cream flavors range from green tea, red bean, and coconut to lychee, mango, and ginger.

Siu Mai is an intriguing-looking steamed bun made from water chestnuts, potatoes, mushrooms, and carrots, decorated by a single green pea. Pot stickers and spring rolls complement dishes such as Buddhist Delight, Yin Yang Fried Rice, and Mushroom Galaxy.

According to the menu, "Many people nowadays are health-conscious about the foods they eat. Eating healthier is the key to long life and youthfulness. In the religion of Buddhism, the holy monks and priests eat only vegetarian foods...."

The Chinese tea houses of old traditionally served tea and dim sum for breakfast, and tea and sweets later in the day. At Kowloon, you can enjoy these treats any time.

KOWLOON
909 Grant Avenue (between Washington and Jackson)
San Francisco, CA 94108

Phone   **(415) 362-9888**

Hours   **Every day, 10:00 a.m.–9:30 p.m.**

Transport	* 1-California, 15-Third, 30-Stockton, 45-Union-Stockton Muni buses * Or, from the Union Square area, walk up Grant Street to Chinatown. Ten Ren Tea is located at 949 Grant Avenue.
Price	
Established	1989

BUDDHIST DELIGHT
YIN YANG FRIED RICE
MUSHROOM GALAXY
DESSERTS
MOON CAKES
DIM SUM
POT OF TEA

"Would you like your adventure now, or tea first?"
"Tea first, quickly!" shouted Wendy.

J. M. Barrie (1860–1937)
Peter Pan

La Nouvelle Patisserie

Indulge in masterpieces of tarts, eclairs, palmiers, marzipan, and cakes in this Parisian-style bakery/café. Jean Yves Duperret, Maître Patissier (a distinguished title bestowed on him by the French government), rises at 4:00 a.m. to begin his day. Though he was once headed for a future in electrical engineering, all that changed when he met his wife, Nelly, who, as it happens, descends from four generations of pastry chefs. After an apprenticeship with her father, Jean Yves was left with a passion for sugar, not circuitry, and today, thousands of sugared roses later, that infatuation is still going strong.

Not surprisingly, the café has the atmosphere of a beehive. Newcomers gawk at the rainbows of strawberries, raspberries, miniature grapes, and kiwis that adorn the tarts like jewels. Others know exactly what they want and point, unashamed, at the mousse and liqueur-drenched sponge cake "deluxe pastries." Some seem torn, unable to decide; they pause before quiche savories (served with green salad and fresh baguette), then eye the precious little bottles of Les Violettes table wine.

"Connoisseur" teas by RYKOFF-SEXTON are served in tall white cups with saucers. The slim selection focuses on black tea standards **Earl Grey** and **English Breakfast,** which are joined by their herbal counterparts, **Chamomile, Lemon Peel,** and **Mint**.

Photos of the bakery's pin-up cakes appear on the walls, and on page after page of The Book of Wedding Cakes. Included in this tome are the usual doves and swans, pastel ribbons of sugar, and even landmarks such as the Golden Gate Bridge and Eiffel Tower. A free tasting and consultation is offered by Nelly for those interested in ordering a wedding cake; call or stop by to make an appointment.

Outdoor seating provides a good view of the fashion parade which passes along Union Street. A satellite La Nouvelle Patisserie is located downtown, at San Francisco Centre.

LA NOUVELLE PATISSERIE
2184 Union Street (at Fillmore)
San Francisco, CA 94123

other San Francisco location:
San Francisco Centre, 865 Market Street, San Francisco, CA
94103 (415) 979-0553

Phone	(415) 931-7655
Hours	Monday–Thursday, 6:30 a.m.–8:00 p.m. Friday and Saturday, 6:30 a.m.–11:00 p.m. Sunday, 8:00 a.m.–7:00 p.m.
Transport	41-Union, 45-Union/Stockton, or 22-Fillmore Muni bus
Price	
Established	1984

 QUICHE SAVORIES
DESSERTS
DELUXE PASTRIES
TARTS
CUP OF TEA

*From five o'clock to eight is on certain occasions a little
eternity; but on such an occasion as this the interval could be
only an eternity of pleasure.*

Henry James (1843–1916)
Portrait of a Lady

SAN FRANCISCO ART INSTITUTE
PETE'S CAFÉ

The ghost of a woman inhabits the tower of this Spanish colonial-style building, which was designed in 1926 by architect Arthur Brown (whose other works include City Hall, Coit Tower, and the War Memorial Opera House). In fact, one can feel her presence sometimes, watching over her flock of artists.

This is not a café for the faint of heart. Reminiscent of a nuclear fallout shelter, it boasts blue plastic-and-metal chairs, long wooden tables (probably meant for sketching upon), and the dizzying pattern of a checkerboard floor. However, due to the Institute's hilltop location, on clear days, sippers are met with a unique panoramic view of the city, the bay, and points beyond. Patio seating is also an option.

BIGELOW teas, poured into white paper cups, include **Darjeeling, Earl Grey, English Teatime** (regular and decaf), **Green, I Love Lemon, Mint Medley, Orange and Spice,** and **Raspberry Royale.** In a large plastic bin marked "**Oolong,**" are a few mysterious-looking FOOJOY tea bags.

Pots and pans hang over the open kitchen, which turns out a colorful array of homemade soups, salads, sandwiches (among them Garden Burgers), and desserts such as cookies (oatmeal chocolate chip and peanut butter) and fudge walnut brownies. Scones (ginger, almond, cranberry, and cherry) tend to sell out early. The incessant rat-a-tat-tat of popcorn from the microwave oven is drowned out by jazz, or any other variety of lively music.

Up-and-coming artists—representing disciplines like digital media, film, painting, photography, printmaking, and sculpture—provide the service, which is irreverent at times, but genuinely friendly. One of the cafe's few decorations is a Walter Keane-style painting of a girl and her guitar—proof that no one here takes themselves too seriously. Student work is exhibited in the Diego Rivera Gallery.

Founded in 1871, the Art Institute's goal is "to provide a training ground for visionary artists." Back in 1946, Ansel Adams founded the photography department. Henri Matisse and Marcel Duchamp both visited the campus. And Janis Joplin herself once worked in the Café.

SAN FRANCISCO ART INSTITUTE
800 Chestnut Street (at Jones)
San Francisco, CA 94133

Phone   (415) 771-7020, Art Institute; (415) 749-4567, Café

Web   http://www.sfai.edu

Hours   Monday–Thursday, 8:00 a.m.–9:00 p.m.
                 Friday, 8:00 a.m.–5:00 p.m.
                 Saturday, 9:00 a.m.–2:00 p.m.
                 Closed Sunday; limited hours during summer
                 and Christmas break.
                 The Diego Rivera Gallery is open daily from
                 9:00 a.m.–5:00 p.m.

Transport   30-Stockton Muni bus or Powell-Mason cable
                 car to Chestnut and Taylor. Walk a block and a
                 half west on Chestnut.

Price

Established   San Francisco Art Institute, 1871. Café, 1969

MENU
GARDEN BURGERS
DESSERTS
SCONES
FUDGE WALNUT BROWNIES
CUP OF TEA

While there is tea, there is hope.

Sir Arthur Wing Pinero (1855–1934)

TAN TAN CAFÉ

The city sky provides a poetic backdrop for tea-drinkers at the Tan Tan Café. Maple cupboards and shelves, a woven wire tea set, and a large, drooping sunflower lend an air of simplicity to this contemporary tea bar.

YAMAMOTOYAMA **Japanese green** tea, served hot or iced, brews in clear Arcoroc teaglasses to a fresh green color, which is soothing in itself. Other options: the Green Tea Float, Green Tea au Lait, and Green Tea au Lait Float. The tea list is rounded out by BIGELOW black teas, **Cinnamon Stick, Constant Comment, Earl Grey, English Teatime, Raspberry Royale,** and herbals, **Apple Orchard, Cranberry Apple, Orange and Spices, Plantation Mint,** and **Sweet Dreams**.

Homemade desserts include Custard Pudding, An Mitsu, (described as a Japanese Jell-O made from seaweed), and a special sweet red bean dessert which is presented in a blue ceramic cup, called Hiyashi Zenzai. But that's not all. There are other temptations: apple tarts, chocolate cream puffs, cakes, and ice cream in fluted bowls — vanilla, strawberry, chocolate, or green tea — which may be drizzled with red bean sauce. Tea-time sandwiches, such as ham and cheese, egg salad, and mixed vegetables, are also offered.

Many Japan Center shoppers visit the Tan Tan Café, taking their tea and sweets "outside," where they sit on white metal folding chairs, and talk among the mall's wispy Ficus trees.

TAN TAN CAFÉ
Kinokuniya Building, Japan Center
1825 Post Street, Suite 223 (between Fillmore and Webster)
San Francisco, CA 94115

Phone	**(415) 346-6260**
Hours	**Every day, 10:00 a.m.–8:00 p.m.**
Transport	**From Union Square, take the westbound 38-Geary Muni bus at Geary and Stockton to Geary**

and Webster, or the westbound 2-Clement, 3-Jackson, or 4-Sutter bus at Sutter and Stockton to Sutter and Webster. From other points, take the 22-Fillmore to Geary and Fillmore. Be sure to visit nearby Kinokuniya Bookstore.

Price

Established   1993

SANDWICHES
DESSERTS
GREEN TEA FLOATS AND GREEN TEA AU LAIT DRINKS
CUP OF TEA
ICED TEA

The outsider may indeed wonder at this seeming much ado about nothing. What a tempest in a teacup! he will say. But when we consider how small after all the cup of human enjoyment is, how soon overflowed with tears, how easily drained to the dregs in our quenchless thirst for infinity, we shall not blame ourselves for making so much of the teacup.

Kakuzo Okakura
The Book of Tea, 1906

TEA-N-CRUMPETS

This is the place if you're a tea-lover in search of scrumptious crumpets to accompany your cuppa. Baker Norman Barahona and his partner, Jena Rose, offer "authentic, handmade, English griddle cakes." You can watch the honeycombed crumpets (which are free of fat, dairy, and preservatives) as they're being made in the storefront bakery. Served plain, with butter, or with soy butter, the crumpets may also be topped with brown sugar and cinnamon, honey, jam, lemon, lime, and orange curd, peanut butter, Nutella, cheddar, ricotta, cream cheese, or maple butter. Other more adventurous, toppings include hard-boiled egg and cheddar, pizza, albacore tuna melt, and cream cheese and smoked salmon.

The **Teas of the Day** selection offers yet more possibilities: **black** (breakfast-style, Earl Grey, and scented), **oolong, green,** and **herbal**. This gives patrons the chance to taste a variety of brands and loose-leaf types, thereby broadening their tea-horizons. TWININGS **Black Currant, Earl Grey, English Breakfast,** and THE REPUBLIC OF TEA **Ginger Peach** and **Mango Ceylon** are the decaffeinated teas.

With the exception of some interesting tea-related photographs, the decor of this crumpet bakery/retail tea shop is no-frills brick-and-wood. Tins of Jacksons of Piccadilly, Royal Garden, Silk Road Teas, and other fine teas, as well as imported curds and preserves (in flavors like greengage and crabapple) line one wall. Teapots and mugs by Pristine Pottery are also for sale. Holiday gift packages, such as Her Majesty's Request (crumpets, Tiptree Preserves, and a tin of Fortnum & Mason tea), would be sure to please the Anglophile on your shopping list.

TEA-N-CRUMPETS
817 Fourth Street (between Lincoln and Cijos)
San Rafael, CA 94901

Phone   (415) 457-2495

Hours   Monday–Friday, 7:30 a.m.–6:00 p.m.
Saturday, 9:00 a.m.–5:30 p.m.
Closed Sunday

Transport   * By car, take Highway 101 north to the Central
San Rafael exit. Turn left on Fourth Street.
* Golden Gate Transit buses #80 (also #70 and
#60) from various Mission Street stops in San
Francisco to downtown San Rafael
Transportation Center. Call (415) 923-2000 for
details.

Price

Established   1994

CRUMPETS
VARIETY OF TOPPINGS
DOUBLE DEVON CLOTTED CREAM
POT OF TEA
CUP OF TEA

*The old philosopher is still among us in the brown coat with
the metal buttons and the shirt which ought to be at the wash,
blinking, puffing, rolling his head, drumming with his fingers,
tearing his meat like a tiger, and swallowing his teas in oceans.*

Lord Thomas Babington Macauley (1800–1859)
The Life of Johnson

TEA LOVERS' RESOURCES

TEA LOVERS' RESOURCES

ASSOCIATIONS

American Botanical Council
P.O. Box 201660
Austin, TX 78720-1660
(512) 331-8868
http://www.herbalgram.org
ABC. A nonprofit organization focused on educating the public about beneficial herbs and plants, such as the Camellia.

American Premium Tea Institute
One World Trade Center
Suite 1210
Long Beach, CA 90831
(562) 624-4190
APTI. Dedicated to "increasing awareness and understanding of the premium tea industry and its products."

American Tea Masters Association
41 Sutter Street, Box 1191
San Francisco, CA 94104
(415) 775-4227
http://www.atma.com
ATMA. Promotes "the pursuit of excellence in the art of tea."

Specialty Tea Registry
420 Lexington Avenue
New York, NY 10170
(212) 986-0250
*ST*R. Formed in 1996; serves the needs of the retail tea industry; a division of the Tea Association of the U.S.A.*

Tea Association of the U.S.A.
420 Lexington Avenue
New York, NY 10170
(212) 986-9415
Founded in 1899; serves the needs of the wholesale tea industry.

The Tea Club
Attention: The Membership Secretary
P.O. Box 221, Guildford
Surrey GU1 3YT
ENGLAND
http://www.teacouncil.co.uk/teaclub.html
Affiliated with the U.K.'s Tea Council; brings together lovers of tea.

The Tea Council
Sir John Lyon House
5 High Timber Street
London EC4V 3NJ
ENGLAND
44-171-248-1024
http://www.teacouncil.co.uk
Promotes tea and tea drinking in the U.K.

Tea Council of the U.S.A.
420 Lexington Avenue
New York, NY 10170
(212) 986-6998
Formed in the 1950s; promotes the tea industry; a division of the Tea Association of the U.S.A.

Urasenke Foundation
2143 Powell Street
San Francisco, CA 94133
(415) 433-6553
http://www.urasenke.or.jp
Perpetuates chanoyu throughout the world.

BOOKS

❋ *Afternoon Tea*
Giordano, Karen. *The Book of Traditional Tea Etiquette.* Langley, WA: Mary Mac's Press, 1996.

Gottlieb, Dawn Hylton, and Diane Sedo. *Taking Tea with Alice: Looking-Glass Tea Parties and Fanciful Victorian Teas.* New York: Warner Treasures/Warner Books, 1997.

Hinley, Sarah, ed. *The Perfect Afternoon Tea Book: A Collection of Teatime Treats.* NY: Lorenz Books/Annes Publishing, Ltd., 1997.

Hynes, Angela. *The Pleasures of Afternoon Tea.* London: HP Books, 1987.

Mackley, Leslie. *The Book of Afternoon Tea.* New York: HP Books/ The Berkley Publishing Group, 1992.

Manchester, Carole. *French Tea: The Pleasures of the Table.* New York: Hearst Books/William Morrow & Company, 1993.

Simpson, Helen. *The London Ritz Book of Afternoon Tea: The Art & Pleasures of Taking Tea.* London: Ebury Press, 1986.

Smith, Michael. *The Afternoon Tea Book.* New York: Atheneum/ The Macmillan Publishing Group, 1986.

✳ Tea Party Recipes

Albright, Barbara, and Leslie Weiner. *Totally Teabreads.* New York: St. Martin's Press, 1994.

Allen, Beth. *A Cozy Book of Tea Time Treats.* Rocklin, CA: Prima Publishing, 1997.

Alston, Elizabeth. *Biscuits and Scones.* New York: Clarkson N. Potter/Random House, 1988.

Berne, Steffi. *The Teatime Cookbook: Tempting Treats and Charming Collectible Teapots.* New York: Villard Books/Random House, 1995.

Cusick, Heidi, ed. *Scones, Muffins and Tea Cakes.* New York: HarperCollins Publishers, 1996.

Foley, Tricia. *Having Tea: Recipes & Table Settings.* New York: Clarkson N. Potter/Random House, 1987.

Greco, Gail. *Tea Time at the Inn: Country Inn Cookbook.* Nashville: Rutledge Hill Press, 1991.

Israel, Andrea. *Taking Tea: The Essential Guide to Brewing, Serving, and Entertaining with Teas from Around the World.* New York: Grove

Weidenfeld, 1988.

Mashiter, Rosa. *A Little Book of English Teas*. San Francisco: Chronicle Books, 1989.

Penner, Lucille. *The Tea Party Book*. New York: Random House Books for Young Readers, 1993.

Pettigrew, Jane. *The National Trust Book of Tea-Time Recipes*. London: The National Trust, 1991.

Richardson, Bruce and Shelley. *A Tea for all Seasons: Celebrating Tea, Art, and Music at the Elmwood Inn*. Louisville, KY: Crescent Hill Books, 1996.

Rubin, Maury. *Book of Tarts*. New York: William Morrow & Company, 1995.

Siegel, Jennifer and Mo. *Celestial Seasonings Cooking with Tea*. New York: Park Lane Press/Random House, 1996.

Tekulsky, Mathew. *Making Your Own Gourmet Tea Drinks*. New York: Crown Publishing Group/Random House, 1995.

❋ *Tea in the East*

Anderson, Jennifer L. *An Introduction to Japanese Tea Ritual*. Albany, NY: State University of New York Press, 1991.

Blofeld, John. *The Chinese Art of Tea*. Boston: Shambhala Publications, 1997.

Chow, Kit, and Ione Kramer. *All the Tea in China*. San Francisco: China Books & Periodicals, 1990.

Hirota, Dennis, ed. *Wind in the Pines: Classic Writing of the Way of Tea as a Buddhist Path*. Fremont, CA: Asian Humanities Press/Jain Publishing Company, 1995.

Koren, Leonard. *Wabi-Sabi for Artists, Designers & Philosophers*. Berkeley, CA: Stone Bridge Press, 1994.

Manchester, Carole. *Tea in the East*. New York: Hearst Books/ William Morrow & Company, 1996.

McClintock, Elizabeth. *The Japanese Tea Garden.* San Francisco: The John McLaren Society, 1977.

Mitscher, M.D., Lester A., and Victoria Dolby. *The Green Tea Book: China's Fountain of Youth.* Garden City Park, NY: Avery Publishing Group, 1997.

Mittwer, Henry. *Zen Flowers: Chabana for the Tea Ceremony.* Rutland, VT: Charles E. Tuttle Company, 1992.

Okakura, Kakuzo. *The Book of Tea.* New York: Kodansha America, 1989 (originally published 1906).

Plutschow, Herbert E. *Historical Chanoyu.* Tokyo: The Japan Times, 1986.

Sadler, A. L. *Cha-no-yu: The Japanese Tea Ceremony.* Rutland, VT: Charles E. Tuttle Company, 1994 (originally published 1933).

Sen XV, Soshitsu. *Chado: The Japanese Way of Tea.* New York: Weatherhill, 1994.

Sen XV, Soshitsu. *Chanoyu: The Urasenke Tradition of Tea.* New York: Weatherhill, 1988.

Tanaka, Sen'o, and Sendo Tanaka. *The Tea Ceremony.* New York: Kodansha America, 1998.

Varley, Paul, and Kumakura Isao, eds. *Tea in Japan: Essays on the History of Chanoyu.* Honolulu: University of Hawaii Press, 1989.

Vitell, Bettina. *The World in a Bowl of Tea: Healthy, Seasonal Foods Inspired by the Japanese Way of Tea.* New York: HarperCollins Publishers, 1997.

Yü, Lu. *The Classic of Tea (Ch'a Ching): Origins & Rituals.* Translated and introduced by Francis Ross Carpenter. Hopewell, N.J.: The Ecco Press, 1995 (originally written in the eighth century).

🌼 Herbal Teas

Fronty, Laura. *Aromatic Teas and Herbal Infusions*. New York: Clarkson N. Potter, Inc./Random House, 1997.

Norman, Jill. *Teas & Tisanes*. New York: Bantam Books, 1989.

Perry, Sara. *The Book of Herbal Teas*. San Francisco: Chronicle Books, 1997.

Toomay, Mindy. *A Cozy Book of Herbal Teas: Recipes, Remedies, and Folk Wisdom*. Rocklin, CA: Prima Publishing, 1995.

🌼 General Reading for Education and Pleasure

Bramah, Edward. *Tea and Coffee: A Modern View of Three Hundred Years of Tradition*. London: Hutchinson Books Ltd./Random House U.K. Ltd., 1972.

Campbell, Dawn L. *The Tea Book*. Gretna, LA: Pelican Books, 1995.

Ministry of Information, The Republic of Tea. *The Book of Tea and Herbs*. Santa Rosa, CA: Cole Publishing Group, 1993.

Pettigrew, Jane. *The Tea Companion: A Connoisseur's Guide*. New York: The Macmillan Publishing Group, 1997.

Podreka, Tomislav. *Serendipitea: A Guide to the Varieties, Origins, and Rituals of Tea*. New York: William Morrow & Company, 1998.

Pratt, James Norwood. *Tea Lover's Treasury*. Introduction by M.F.K. Fisher. Santa Rosa, CA: Cole Publishing Group, 1982.

Pratt, James Norwood, with Diana Rosen. *The Tea Lover's Companion: The Ultimate Connoisseur's Guide to Buying, Brewing, and Enjoying Tea*. New York: Carol Publishing Group, 1996.

Resnick, Jane. *Loving Tea: The Tea Lover's Guide*. NY: Berkley Books/Berkley Publishing Group/Penguin Putnam, 1997.

Sach, Penelope. *On Tea and Healthy Living*. St. Leonard's, Australia: Allen & Unwin Pty. Ltd., 1995.

Schapira, Joel, David, and Karl. *The Book of Coffee & Tea*. New

York: St. Martin's Press, 1996.

Stella, A., and N. Beauthéac, G. Brochard, and C. Donzel. *The Book of Tea*. Translated by Deke Dusinberre. Preface by Anthony Burgess. Paris: Flammarion, 1992.

Ukers, William H. *All About Tea*. Westport, CT: Hyperion Press, 1994 (originally published 1935).

Ukers, William H. *The Romance of Tea*. New York: Alfred A. Knopf, 1936.

Wild, Antony. *The East India Company Book of Tea*. New York: HarperCollins Publishers, 1994.

Woodward, Nancy Hyden. *Teas of the World*. New York: Collier Books/The Macmillan Publishing Group, 1980.

✳ *Tea Memoirs*

Barnes, Emilie. *If Teacups Could Talk: Sharing a Cup of Kindness with Treasured Friends*. Eugene, OR: Harvest House Publishers, 1994.

Goodwin, Jason Scott. *A Time for Tea*. New York: Random House, 1991.

Gustafson, Helen. *The Agony of the Leaves: The Ecstasy of My Life with Tea*. New York: Henry Holt & Company, 1996.

Guth, Christine M. E. *Art, Tea and Industry: Masuda Takashi and the Mitsui Circle*. Princeton, New Jersey: Princeton University Press, 1993.

Rivers, Michele. *Time for Tea: Tea and Conversation with Thirteen English Women*. New York: Crown Publishing Group/Random House, 1995.

Sen XV, Soshitsu. *Tea Life, Tea Mind*. New York: Weatherhill, 1995.

Twining, Sam. *All the Tea in China*. Andover, MA: R. Twining & Company, 1992 (originally published 1900).

❋ *Inspiring Tea Books*

Bender, Lois. *Tea Quotes: A Journal of Tea, Inner Beauty and Well-Being*. New York: Lois Bender Design, 1995.

Emmerson, Robin. *British Teapots & Tea Drinking*. London: HMSO Press, n.d.

Engelbreit, Mary. *Time for Tea*. Kansas City, MO: Andrews & McMeel, 1997.

Gray, Arthur. *A Perfect Cup of Tea*. Ed. Pat Ross. San Francisco: Chronicle Books, 1995 (originally published 1903).

A Highland Seer. *Reading Tea Leaves*. Introduction by James Norwood Pratt. Afterword by John Harney. New York: Crown Publishing Group/Random House, 1995.

Holt, Geraldine. *A Cup of Tea: Treasures for Teatime*. London: Pavilion Books Ltd., 1981.

Isles, Joanna. *A Proper Tea*. London: Piatkus Books, 1987.

King, M. Dalton. *Tea Time: Tradition, Presentation, and Recipes*. Philadelphia, PA: Running Press Book Publishers, 1992.

Kirk, David. *Miss Spider's Tea Party*. New York: Scholastic, 1994.

Knight, Elizabeth. *Tea with Friends*. Pownal, VT: Storey Books, 1998.

Koch, Maryjo. *Tea: Delectables for All Seasons*. San Francisco: Swans Island Books/Collins Publishers San Francisco/HarperCollins Publishers, 1996.

McCormick, Malachi. *A Decent Cup of Tea*. New York: Clarkson N. Potter/Random House, 1991.

Perry, Sara. *The Tea Book*. San Francisco: Chronicle Books, 1993.

Slavin, Sara, and Karl Petzke. *Tea: Essence of the Leaf*. San Francisco: Chronicle Books, 1998.

Stoddard, Alexandra. *Tea Celebrations: The Way to Serenity*. New

York: William Morrow & Company, 1994.

Tippett, Paul. *Teapots: The Connoisseur's Guide* (from the Christie's Collectibles series). Boston, MA: Bulfinch Press/Little, Brown & Company, 1996.

Victoria magazine editors. *The Charms of Tea: Reminiscences and Recipes.* New York: Hearst Books/William Morrow & Company, 1991.

MAGAZINES AND NEWSLETTERS

coffee journal — America's Gourmet Coffee & Tea Guide
123 North Third Street, Suite 508
Minneapolis, MN 55401
(612) 338-4125
Colorful and well-written; elevates both beverages to a new level of appreciation.

HerbalGram
P.O. Box 201660
Austin, TX 78720-1660
(512) 331-8868
A quarterly publication of the American Botanical Council.

Matsukaze — Chanoyu Journal for the Urasenke Foundation, North America
2143 Powell Street
San Francisco, CA 94133
(415) 433-6553
Offers "a glimpse of the arts and philosophies that chanoyu synthesizes so beautifully."

Tea, A Magazine
P.O. Box 348
Scotland, CT 06264
(860) 456-1145
Cozy and appealing; focuses on "tea's significance in art, history, literature, and society."

Tea & Coffee Trade Journal
130 West 42nd Street, Suite 1050

New York, NY 10036
(212) 391-2060
"The international voice of the tea and coffee industry since 1901." A bit dry for the average reader, but a good reference tool for those interested in the tea business.

The Tea Quarterly
2118 Wilshire Boulevard, Suite 634
Santa Monica, CA 90403
(310) 479-7370
A national journal of tea; refined and tasteful.

Tea Talk — A Newsletter on the Pleasures of Tea
P.O. Box 860
Sausalito, CA 94966
(415) 331-1557
Chatty and full of national tea news, lore, and the occasional recipe.

PROTOCOL SCHOOL

The Protocol School of Washington
International Headquarters
1401 Chain Bridge Road, Suite 202
McLean, Virginia 22101
(703) 821-5613
http://www.psow.com
Train to be a tea etiquette consultant!

TEA CEREMONY CLASSES, WORKSHOPS, AND CELEBRATIONS

↜ JAPANESE TEA CEREMONY (ORGANIZATIONS)

Green Gulch Farm Zen Center
1601 Shoreline Highway
Sausalito, CA 94965
(415) 383-3134

Urasenke Foundation
2143 Powell Street
San Francisco, CA 94133
(415) 433-6553

〜 JAPANESE TEA CEREMONY (INDIVIDUALS)

David Furukawa Chen
Musoan Tea House
665 Geary Street, #402
San Francisco, CA 94102
(415) 440-9833

Kikuyo Sekino
c/o Nichi Bei Kai Cultural Center
1759 Sutter Street
San Francisco, CA 94115
(415) 921-1782 or (415) 751-9676

Kimika Soko Takechi and Larry Sokyo Tiscornia
(415) 752-6944
e-mail: teatimes@sirius.com
http://www.pacific-bridge-arts.com/TeaMasters

〜 CHINESE TEA CEREMONY (INDIVIDUALS)

Kathi Wong
c/o Side by Side
163 Main Street
San Francisco, CA 94105
(415) 243-8083

TEA SHOPS

SPECIALIZING IN FINE LOOSE-LEAF TEAS

A'Cuppa Tea
Crocker Galleria, Second Level
50 Post Street
San Francisco, CA 94104
(415) 986-9958
Creative gourmet teas.

Freed Teller & Freed
1326 Polk Street, San Francisco, CA 94109
(415) 673-0922 (also mail order)
Embarcadero Center, West Tower, San Francisco, CA 94111
(415) 986-8851
One of San Francisco's first tea shops.

Imperial Tea Court
1411 Powell Street
San Francisco, CA 94133
(415) 788-6080 (also mail order)
http://www.imperialtea.com
Owner Roy Fong is known in tea circles for his Monkey-Picked Ti Kuan Yin.

Lisa's Tea Treasures
1145 Merrill Street, Menlo Park, CA 94025 (650) 326-8327
1875 South Bascom Avenue, Campbell, CA 95008 (408) 371-7377
330 N. Santa Cruz Avenue, Los Gatos, CA 95030 (408) 395-8327
71 Lafayette Circle, Lafayette, CA 94549 (510) 283-2226
(800) 500-4TEA (mail order)
http://www.lisasteas.com
Featuring Tea Princess teas.

Peaberry's Coffee & Tea
5655 College Avenue
Oakland, CA 94618
(510) 653-0450 or (510) 420-0473 (mail order)
An intriguing selection, such as Willow Leaf Bancha, Cameronian, and Rose Petal Tea.

Peet's Coffee & Tea
2257 Market Street (and other locations throughout S.F. and the Bay Area)
San Francisco, CA 94114
(415) 626-6416 or (800) 999-2132 (mail order)
http://www.peets.com
"The finest estate-produced teas."

Side by Side
163 Main Street
San Francisco, CA 94105
(415) 243-8083

Look for Tea Master's Blends and other fine teas from The Golden Tearoom.

Tea & Company
2207 Fillmore Street
San Francisco, CA 94115
(415) 929-TEAS or (888) 832-4884 (mail order)
For teas that will "astound your palate."

Tea Time
542 Ramona Street
Palo Alto, CA 94301
(650) 32T-CUPS or (877) 32T-CUPS (mail order)
http://www.tea-time.com
Varietal teas for the neophyte and the experienced tea-drinker.

Ten Ren Tea
949 Grant Avenue
San Francisco, CA 94108
(415) 362-0656 or (800) 292-2049 (mail order)
A Chinese tea emporium, whose name means "heavenly love."

Mail-Order Tea

SPECIALIZING IN FINE LOOSE-LEAF TEAS, TEAWARE, AND OTHER ITEMS

Choice Organic Teas
Granum, Inc.
2901 N.E. Blakeley
Seattle, WA 98105
(206) 525-0051
Certified organic teas from gardens in India, Sri Lanka, Japan, East Africa, Europe, and the Pacific Northwest.

Grace Tea Company
50 West 17th Street
New York, NY 10011
(212) 255-2935
"The connoisseur's cup of tea." Try their innovative teapot filters.

Harney & Sons
P.O. Box 638

Salisbury, CT 06068
(888) HARNEY-T/427-6398
http://www.harney.com
*Served at many luxury hotels. The Harney clan's colorful catalogue,
featuring some of the world's best teas, is inspiring in itself.*

The Honorable Jane Company
P.O. Box 35
Potter Valley, CA 95469-0035
e-mail: davepeg@pacific.net
Gardeners note: This is a source for the Camellia sinensis *plant.*

Leaves · Pure Teas
1392 Lowrie Avenue
South San Francisco, CA 94080
(415) 583-1157
http://www.leaves.com
"Real ingredients strong enough to stand on their own."

Lipton
P.O. Box 3000
Grand Rapids, MN 55745
(800) 697-7887
*A perennial, with its roots in the grocery store business. When in
Pasadena, visit the new Lipton Teahouse.*

Mark T. Wendell, Importer
P.O. Box 1312
West Concord, Massachusetts 01742
(978) 369-3709
http://www.lsiweb.com/marktwendell
*This company's beginnings can be traced back to 1852. Aside from their
own blends, they offer Indar, Ty·Phoo, PG Tips, Melroses, and Sushi
Chef.*

Masala Chai
P.O. Box 8375
Santa Cruz, CA 95061
(408) 426-CHAI
First of its kind; now mainly wholesale. Try their "aphroteasiac" chai.

O'Mona International Tea Company
6 South Main Street

Port Chester, New York 10573
(914) 937-8858
*This "World Tea House" catalogue offers brands not found elsewhere,
such as Davison Newman & Co., Douwe Egberts, and Kousmichoff.*

The Republic of Tea
8 Digital Drive, Suite 100
Novato, CA 94949
(800) 298-4TEA
http://www.sipbysip.com
Their mission: "To create a Tea Revolution."

San Francisco Herb Co.
250 14th Street
San Francisco, CA 94103
(415) 861-7174 or (800) 227-4530
http://www.sfherb.com
*Wholesale herbs, spices, teas, and potpourri. Visit their showroom at
14th and Mission, or their Internet "warehouse."*

Sarum Teas
P.O. Box 479
Salisbury, Connecticut 06068
(800) 342-1922
A gourmet tea company founded by the son of a London tea merchant.

Satori Teas
825 West Market Street
Salinas, CA 93901
(800) 444-7286
http://www.satoriteas.com/menu.html
Organic tea company, involved in herbal activism.

Silk Road Teas
P.O. Box 287
Lagunitas, CA 94938
(415) 488-9017
Fine and rare Chinese teas – from white to Pu-erh. Organic.

Simpson & Vail
P.O. Box 765
Brookfield, CT 06804
(800) 282-TEAS

http://www.svtea.com
*Since 1929. Their catalogue, which features an organic first flush
Darjeeling from the Ambootia Estate, reads like a "Who's Who" of tea.*

Stash Tea
9040 SW Burnham Street
Tigard, OR 97223
(800) 826-4218
http://www.stashtea.com
*1997 marked Stash Tea's 25th anniversary in the world of tea.
Adventurous sippers will want to try their Exotica tea bags.*

Steep Co.
P.O. Box 89
South Glastonbury, CT 06073
(800) STEEPCO
http://www.steep.com
State-of-the-art teas for Generation X.

Tazo
P.O. Box 66
Portland, OR 97207
(800) 299-9445
"The Reincarnation of Tea." Not your ordinary tea company.

The Tea Club/Spice of the Month
M. B. Thomas & Co.
1715 North Burling Street
Chicago, IL 60614
(888) TEA-SHOP
Members receive two different teas each month.

The Tea Company
Wood Island, Suite 210
60 E. Sir Frances Drake Boulevard
Larkspur, CA 94939
(415) 925-9936
The tea of choice at the Mark Hopkins and Neiman Marcus.

Tea Importers
47 Riverside Avenue
Westport, CT 06880
(203) 226-3301

Loose-leaf black teas from China, Taiwan, Sri Lanka, and Rwanda,
packed in small wooden chests.

Triple Leaf Tea
434 N. Canal Street, Unit 5
South San Francisco, CA 94080
(650) 588-8258 or (800) 552-7448
http://www.tripleleaf-tea.com
"Authentic traditional Chinese medicinal teas."

Upton Tea Imports
231 South Street
Hopkinton, MA 01748
(800) 234-8327
"Purveyors of the world's finest teas."

Water and Leaves
P.O. Box 7228
Redwood City, CA 94063
(888) 517-3199
http://www.wayoftea.com
"Follow the leaves down your own path of discovery." Chinese teas, tea
music, and "guardian of water" teapots.

TEA-TIME EDIBLES

🌿 BRITISH AFTERNOON TEAS & SPECIAL TEA OCCASIONS

Alfred Schilling
1695 Market Street
San Francisco, CA 94103
(415) 431-8447
Chocolates and truffles in the forms of cherubs, pyramids, and
butterflies.

Ashbury Market
205 Frederick Street
San Francisco, CA 94117
(415) 566-3134
Freshly baked scones by Raison d'être.

The Butler's Pantry
305 2nd Street
Los Altos, CA 94022
(650) 941-9676
Biscuits and marmalade.

Cost Plus World Market
2552 Taylor Street
San Francisco, CA 94133
(415) 928-6200
Teas, shortbread, scone mix, and Elizabethan curds.

Draeger's Market Place
222 E. Fourth Avenue
San Mateo, CA 94401
(650) 685-3700
Everything from freshly baked scones and tarts to teas, champagne, McVitie's digestive biscuits, and Somerdale double Devon clotted cream.

Epicure Shop
Neiman Marcus
150 Stockton Street, Fourth Floor
San Francisco, CA 94108
(415) 362-3900
British teas, oatcakes, and Somerdale double Devon clotted cream. Also fine chocolates and caviar.

Garden Court
Palace Hotel
2 New Montgomery Street
San Francisco, CA 94105
(415) 512-1111
Ask about their regal selection of teas, herbal infusions, jams, and gift sets. Tiaras, crowns, and candied scepters also sold.

I Love Chocolate
397 Arguello Boulevard
San Francisco, CA 94118
(415 750-9460
Freshly baked scones, tarts, etc.

It's Delectable
4416 18th Street
San Francisco, CA 94114

(415) 565-0280
Freshly baked scones, tarts, etc.

Joseph Schmidt Confections
3489 16th Street
San Francisco, CA 94114
(415) 861-8682
Divine chocolates and truffles.

Just Desserts
248 Church Street (and other locations in S.F., Berkeley, Oakland, and Palo Alto)
San Francisco, CA 94114
(415) 626-5774
Freshly baked scones, tarts, etc.

Lady Pierrepont's
1205 Howard Avenue
Burlingame, CA 94010
(650) 342-6065
Fortnum & Mason teas, jellies of gooseberry and quince, Walker's shortbread, and other edibles.

La Nouvelle Patisserie
2184 Union Street, San Francisco, CA 94123 (415) 931-7655
San Francisco Centre, 865 Market Street, San Francisco, CA 94103
(415) 979-0553
Freshly baked scones, tarts, etc.

Noe Valley Bakery & Bread Co.
4073 24th Street
San Francisco, CA 94114
(415) 550-1405
Freshly baked scones, tarts, etc.

Now & Zen
1826 Buchanan Street
San Francisco, CA 942115
(415) 922-9696
Vegan baked goods.

Rock of Gibraltar
1026 Alma Street
Menlo Park, CA 94025

(650) 325-8981
Featuring The Garden Grill's homemade treats and British loose-leaf teas.

Tassajara Bread Bakery
1000 Cole Street
San Francisco, CA 94117
(415) 664-8947
Freshly baked Irish soda muffins, scones, tarts, etc.

Tea-n-Crumpets
817 Fourth Street
San Rafael, CA 94901
(415) 457-2495
Teas, freshly baked crumpets, and preserves.

The Village Green
89 Avenue Portola
El Granada, CA 94018
(650) 726-3690
Homemade lemon curd, and "crisps."

〜 JAPANESE TEA CEREMONIES & SPECIAL TEA OCCASIONS

Asakichi
1730 Geary Boulevard, Suites 108, 204, 206, and 206B
Kinokuniya Building
Japan Center
San Francisco, CA 94115
(415) 921-2147
Fresh powdered green tea (matcha)*, whisks, incense, etc.*

Japanese Tea Garden
Hagiwara Tea Garden Drive
Golden Gate Park
San Francisco, CA 94117
(415) 752-1171
Green teas and assorted snacks.

Yamada Seika Confectionery
1955 Sutter Street
San Francisco, CA 94115
(415) 922-3848

Seasonal bean cakes (manju).

🍃 CHINESE TEA CEREMONIES & SPECIAL TEA OCCASIONS

Golden Gate Fortune Cookies
56 Ross Alley
San Francisco, CA 94108
781-3956
Custom-make fortune cookies. Stop by for a tour of the factory!

Kowloon Vegetarian Restaurant
909 Grant Avenue
San Francisco, CA 94108
(415) 362-9888
Dim sum and sweet Moon Cakes.

Mee Mee Bakery
1328 Stockton Street
San Francisco, CA 94133
(415) 362-3204
Custom-made fortune cookies.

🍃 INDIAN-STYLE TEAS & SPECIAL TEA OCCASIONS

New Bombay Bazaar
548 Valencia Street
San Francisco, CA 94110
(415) 621-1717
Indian foods and spices.

Rainbow Grocery & General Store
1745 Folsom Street
San Francisco, CA 94103
(415) 863-0620
Various types of chai.

🍃 MIDDLE EASTERN-STYLE TEAS & SPECIAL TEA OCCASIONS

Haig's Delicacies
642 Clement Street
San Francisco, CA 94118
(415) 752-6283
Baklava, halvah, and other exotic sweets.

Cinderella
436 Balboa Street
San Francisco, CA 94118
(415) 751-9690
Freshly baked butter cookies, cakes, etc.

TEAWARE

A'Cuppa Tea
Crocker Galleria, Second Level
50 Post Street
San Francisco, CA 94104
(415) 986-9958
Colorful ceramics, Moller tea kettles, and stylish tea towels.

Asakichi
1730 Geary Boulevard
Suites 108 and 206B
Kinokuniya Building
Japan Center
San Francisco, CA 94115
(415) 921-2147
Lovely cast iron teapots.

Asian Exhibition Kiosk
Asian Art Museum
Golden Gate Park
San Francisco, CA 94118
(415) 379-8800
Yixing teapots and bamboo tea scoops.

The Butler's Pantry
305 2nd Street
Los Altos, CA 94022
(650) 941-9676
British-style teaware, such as "hunt" mugs and Regency bone china.

Chai
25 Ward Street

Larkspur, CA 94939
(415) 945-7161
Artsy teapots and tea paraphernalia.

The Conversation Piece
889 Santa Cruz Avenue
Menlo Park, CA 94025
(650) 327-9101
Second-hand teacups and Lomonosov Russian teaware.

Cornelia Park
183 Stanford Shopping Center
Palo Alto, CA 94304
(650) 327-0977
MacKenzie-Childs teapots of every stripe and color.

Cost Plus World Market
2552 Taylor Street
San Francisco, CA 94133
(415) 928-6200
Pristine Pottery and Bodum teapots; whistling tea kettles.

Do Dah Days
1185 Church Street
San Francisco, CA 94114
(415) 647-4775
Teacups and other curios.

Draeger's Market Place
222 E. Fourth Avenue
San Mateo, CA 94401
(650) 685-3700
An array of classic Brown Betty, cast iron, porcelain, stainless steel, and Yixing teapots.

Epicure Shop & Gift Gallery
Neiman Marcus
150 Stockton Street, Fourth Floor
San Francisco, CA 94108
(415) 362-3900
MacKenzie-Childs whimsical teaware, modern Alessi teapots, and "recycled" British hotel ware.

Freed Teller & Freed
1326 Polk Street, San Francisco, CA 94109 (415) 673-0922
Embarcadero Center, West Tower, San Francisco, CA 94111
(415) 986-8851
Brown Betty, assorted bone china, and Yixing teapots. Also Swiss gold tea infusers.

Genji Antiques
22 Peace Plaza, Suite 190
Japan Center
San Francisco, CA 94115
(415) 931-1616
Traditional Japanese antiques, such as tsukubai, *and decorative teapots.*

Gump's
135 Post Street
San Francisco, CA 94108
(415) 982-1616
Four-hundred china patterns from which to choose!

Imperial Tea Court
1411 Powell Street
San Francisco, CA 94133
(415) 788-6080
Yixing teapots, gaiwan, *bamboo implements, and special tea sets.*

Japanese Tea Garden
Hagiwara Tea Garden Drive
Golden Gate Park
San Francisco, CA 94117
(415) 752-1171
The odd porcelain teapot.

Lady Pierrepont's
1205 Howard Avenue
Burlingame, CA 94010
(650) 342-6065
Silver heirlooms, and lace from Nottingham.

Lady Sybil's Closet
1484 Church Street
San Francisco, CA 94131
(415) 282-2088

Vintage laces, linens, and embroideries.

Laurel Street Antiques & Collectibles
671 Laurel Street
San Carlos, CA 94070
(650) 593-1152
Silver, china, and linens.

Lisa's Tea Treasures
1145 Merrill Street, Menlo Park, CA 94025 (650) 326-8327
1875 South Bascom Avenue, Campbell, CA 95008 (408) 371-7377
330 N. Santa Cruz Avenue, Los Gatos, CA 95030 (408) 395-8327
71 Lafayette Circle, Lafayette, CA 94549 (510) 283-2226
"A tea-lover's dream." Quaint accoutrements, and teapots imported from England, Germany, Russia, China, and Japan.

Lovejoy's
1185 Church Street
San Francisco, CA 94114
(415) 648-5895
Antique teacups and saucers, also tea and clotted cream.

Lucy's Tea House
180 Castro Street
Mountain View, CA 94041
(650) 969-6365
Yixing teapots.

Mikado
889 Santa Cruz Avenue
Menlo Park, CA 94025
(650) 321-4560
Cast iron teapots.

Museum Store
California Palace of the Legion of Honor
390 Legion of Honor Drive
Lincoln Park
San Francisco, CA 94121
(415) 750-3677
An eclectic collection, including Spode, Lomonosov, and Roji teaware.

Museum Store
De Young Museum
75 Tea Garden Drive
Golden Gate Park
San Francisco, CA 94118
(415) 750-3642
Woodmere's elegant White House Dessert Collection china, Heath ceramic teapots, and museum replica teapot pins.

Museum Store
San Francisco Museum of Modern Art
151 Third Street
San Francisco, CA 94103
(415) 357-4035
Contemporary teaware of glass and stainless steel.

Peaberry's Coffee & Tea
5655 College Avenue
Oakland, CA 94618
(510) 653-0450
Bodum, Sadler, and Pristine Pottery teapots.

Peet's Coffee & Tea
2257 Market Street (and other locations throughout S.F. and the Bay Area)
San Francisco, CA 94114
(415) 626-6416
Tea kettles, Bodum teapots, and assorted ceramics.

Pullman & Co.
108 Throckmorton Avenue
Mill Valley, CA 94941
(415) 383-0847
Unusual teapots and other home furnishings.

Red & Green Company
2011 Market Street, Suite 5
San Francisco, CA 94114
(415) 626-1375
Exquisite Yixing teapots, gaiwan, *and jade cups.*

Sean's Antiques
2501 Irving Street

San Francisco, CA 94122
(415) 731-0758
Silver and china.

Swanson Gallery
Fairmont Hotel
950 Mason Street
San Francisco, CA 94108
(415) 433-4802
Iron, bronze, and Yixing teapots, and other treasures.

Tai Yick Trading Co.
1400 Powell Street
San Francisco, CA 94133
(415) 986-0961
Porcelain teapots and inspiring statuary.

Tea & Company
2207 Fillmore Street
San Francisco, CA 94115
(415) 929-TEAS
Bodum and Yixing teapots, and tea paraphernalia.

Tea-n-Crumpets
817 Fourth Street
San Rafael, CA 94901
(415) 457-2495
Pristine Pottery teapots.

Tea Time
542 Ramona Street
Palo Alto, CA 94301
(650) 32T-CUPS
*Chatsford teapots with built-in infusers, vintage teacups, and
Lomonosov Russian teaware.*

Telegraph Hill Antiques
580 Union Street
San Francisco, CA 94133
(415) 982-7055
Silver and china, some from the Victorian era, and British tea caddies.

Ten Ren Tea
949 Grant Avenue
San Francisco, CA 94108
(415) 362-0656
Yixing teapots.

The Village Green
89 Avenue Portola
El Granada, CA 94018
(650) 726-3690
Crownford teapots, cozies, and assorted bone china.

Virginia Breier
3091 Sacramento Street
San Francisco, CA 94115
(415) 929-7173
Non-traditional contemporary teapots.

VIRTUAL TEA

INTERESTING AND UNUSUAL WEB SITES

The Book of Tea **by Kakuzo Okakura**
http://www.teatime.com/tea/TheBookOfTea/index.phtml
Electronic edition of the classic.

Chado
http://www.art.uiuc.edu/tea/main.html
The way of tea (in the middle of the cornfields).

Chinese Tea Ceremony
http://desires.com/1.4/Food/Docs/tea.html
The true story of San Lee, apprentice teamaster.

Hello Kitty's Tea Party
http://www.groovygames.com/kitty
A tea party with Kitty; aimed at children.

Himalayan Tea Garden
http://www.ipass.net/~htg
A visit to a tea estate; recipes.

Japanese Green Tea
http://www.daisan.co.jp/cha2e.htm
Origins and health aspects.

Maruichi Green Tea Farm
http://www.maruichi-jp.com/e_index.htm
A behind-the-scenes look at an actual tea farm.

"A Nice Cup of Tea" by George Orwell
http://cns-web.bu.edu/pub/snorraso/tea/tea-George-Orwell.html
Orwell's golden rules about tea, originally published in 1946.

The Perfect Pot of Tea (tay)
http://www.ncf.carleton.ca/~bj333/HomePage.tea.html
Friendly advice from Conrad Jay Bladey about the Irish tea ritual.

Puppet that Serves Tea
http://www.cjn.or.jp/karakuri/serve-tea-1.html
Complete with teacup and tray; one of many.

Russian Tea Ceremony
http://www.teaware.com
A unique collection of teaware by artist Julie Kirillova.

The Tea Association
http://home.sol.no/cbugge/index.html
Uniting tea-lovers on the web; look for the Twinings tea bag.

Tea Hyakka Magazine
http://www.teahyakka.com
Inspiring; to enter, click on "English" in picture of Rikyû.

The Tea Page
http://hjem.get2net.dk/bnielsen
From Denmark: Birger Nielsen's informative web site.

Welcome to the World of Japanese Tea Ceremony
http://www.nakajimak.co.jp/index2.html
Good graphics. Includes a discussion of history and manners.

USEFUL PHONE NUMBERS

∽ TRANSPORT

AC Transit	(510) 817-1717
BART	(510) 464-6000
CalTrain	(800) 660-4287
Golden Gate Transit (bus)	(415) 923-2000
Golden Gate Transit (ferry)	(415) 923-2308
Marguerite Shuttle	(650) 723-9362
Muni	(415) 673-MUNI
Yellow Cab (S.F.)	(415) 626-2345

∽ PARKING GARAGES

NOB HILL

Crocker Garage   (415) 346-5565
1045 California Street
for Fairmont, Mark Hopkins, and Stanford Court Hotels

Masonic Temple Garage   (415) 474-1567
1101 California Street
for Fairmont, Mark Hopkins, and Stanford Court Hotels

DOWNTOWN

Embarcadero Garage #1   (415) 772-0676
Battery Street (between Clay and Sacramento)
for Park Hyatt Hotel

Hearst Parking Center   (415) 989-4000
45 Third Street
for Palace Hotel

Saint Mary's Square Garage   (415) 956-8106
651 California Street
for Ritz-Carlton Hotel

Union Square Garage   (415) 397-0631
333 Post Street
for St. Francis Hotel and Neiman Marcus

INDEX

A'Cuppa Tea, 110
Alfred Schilling, 144

Barnes & Noble, 146
Borders, 148
Butler's Pantry, 58

Café Andrea, 120
Café Hana, 150
California Palace of the
    Legion of Honor, 152
Chai of Larkspur, 123
Chez Panisse, 127
Cinderella, 154

De Young Museum, 156
Draeger's Market Place, 158

Elizabeth F. Gamble
    Garden Center, 130
English Rose, 60

Fairmont Hotel, 29

Garden Grill, 63
Grace Cathedral, 161
Green Gulch Farm
    Zen Center, 88
Greens, 163

I Love Chocolate, 165
Imperial Tea Court, 91

Japanese Tea Garden, 95
Just Desserts, 167

King George Hotel, 66
Kowloon, 170

Lady Pierrepont's, 70
La Nouvelle Patisserie, 172
Lisa's Tea Treasures, 73
Lovejoy's, 76
Lucy's Tea House, 99

Mad Magda's, 133
Mark Hopkins Hotel, 32

Neiman Marcus, 35
O Chamé, 135

Palace Hotel, 37
Park Hyatt Hotel, 42

Renaissance Stanford
    Court Hotel, 46
Ritz-Carlton Hotel, 49

San Francisco Art
    Institute, 174
San Francisco Museum
    of Modern Art, 138
Side by Side, 103
St. Francis Hotel, 53

Tal-y-Tara, 81
Tan Tan Café, 176
Tea & Company, 113
Tea-n-Crumpets, 178
Tea Time, 116

Urasenke Foundation, 105

Village Green, 84

ACKNOWLEDGMENTS

Grateful acknowledgment is made to the following for permission to reprint quotes and illustrations:

QUOTES
Pages 14 and 17, from THE CLASSIC OF TEA (by Lu Yü) by Francis R. Carpenter. Copyright © 1974 by Francis R. Carpenter (translation). By permission of Little, Brown and Company.
Page 23, by Horace Bristol, courtesy of the estate of Horace Bristol and *The Tea Quarterly*, Volume X, Number 11, Issue 14, 1997.
Page 104, from THE CLASSIC OF TEA (by Lu Yü) by Francis R. Carpenter. Copyright © 1974 by Francis R. Carpenter (translation). By permission of Little, Brown and Company.
Pages 106 and 107, from an essay by Sen Soshitsu XV, as translated in *Matsukaze — Chanoyu Journal for the Ursasenke Foundation, North America*, Issue No. 9, Summer 1997.
Page 161, by the Reverend Dr. Lauren Artress, courtesy of *Source, A Publication of Veriditas: The Worldwide Labyrinth Project*.

ILLUSTRATIONS
Cover art courtesy of Cavallini & Co., San Francisco.
Page 28, courtesy of The Fairmont Hotel.
Page 38, courtesy of the San Francisco History Center, San Francisco Public Library.
Page 39, courtesy of the Sheraton Palace Hotel.
Page 44, courtesy of the Park Hyatt Hotel, photo by Kingmond Young.
Page 50, courtesy of The Ritz-Carlton Hotel, San Francisco.
Page 61, copyright © 1997 by Phyllis Christopher.
Page 67, courtesy of the King George Hotel.
Page 77, copyright © 1998 by Ulrica Hume.
Page 78, copyright © 1998 by Ulrica Hume.
Page 97, courtesy of the San Francisco History Center, San Francisco Public Library.
Page 102, copyright © RMN, photo by Jean Schormans of the original photo by Lewis Carroll.
Page 112, courtesy of Tea & Company.
Page 124, courtesy of Chai of Larkspur, photo by Greg West.
Page 139, copyright © 1994 by SFMOMA/Richard Barnes.
page 155, courtesy of the Fine Arts Museums of San Francisco.
Page 159, courtesy of the Draeger family.
Page 162, labyrinth icon courtesy of *Source, A Publication of Veriditas: The Worldwide Labyrinth Project*.
Pages 214 and 215, maps copyright © 1998 by Ulrica Hume.

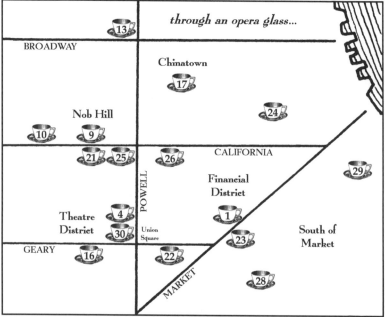

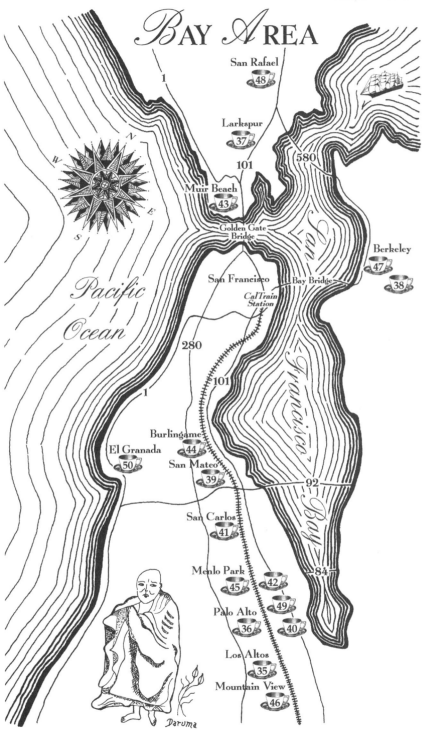

BAY AREA

San Rafael
48

Larkspur
37

101

580

Muir Beach
43

Golden Gate
Bridge

Berkeley
47

38

San Francisco

Bay Bridge

CalTrain
Station

Pacific

Ocean

280

101

1

Burlingame
44

El Granada
50

San Mateo
39

92

San Carlos
41

84

Menlo Park
45   42

49

Palo Alto
36   40

Los Altos
35

Mountain View
46

San Francisco Bay

Daruma

•L e g e n d•

SAN FRANCISCO

1 A'Cuppa Tea
2 Alfred Schilling
3 Barnes & Noble
4 Borders
5 Café Hana
6 California Palace of the
  Legion of Honor
7 Cinderella
8 De Young Museum
9 Fairmont Hotel
10 Grace Cathedral
11 Greens
12 I Love Chocolate
13 Imperial Tea Court

14 Japanese Tea Gardens
15 Just Desserts
16 King George Hotel
17 Kowloon
18 La Nouvelle Patisserie
19 Lovejoy's
20 Mad Magda's
21 Mark Hopkins Hotel
22 Neiman Marcus
23 Palace Hotel
24 Park Hyatt Hotel
25 Renaissance Stanford
  Court Hotel

26 Ritz-Carlton Hotel
27 San Francisco Art
  Institute
28 San Francisco Museum
  of Modern Art
29 Side by Side
30 St. Francis Hotel
31 Tal-y-Tara
32 Tan Tan Café
33 Tea & Company
34 Urasenke Foundation

BAY AREA

35 The Butler's Pantry
36 Café Andrea
37 Chai of Larkspur
38 Chez Panisse
39 Draeger's Market
  Place
40 Elizabeth F. Gamble
  Garden Center

41 The English Rose
42 The Garden Grill
43 Green Gulch Farm
  Zen Center
44 Lady Pierrepont's
45 Lisa's Tea Treasures

46 Lucy's Tea House
47 O Chamé
48 Tea-n-Crumpets
49 Tea Time
50 The Village Green

TEA NOTES

Use these pages to record your favorite tea experiences...

𝒰lrica ℋume is a fiction and travel writer, a native Bay Arean, and tea devotee. She has written about the tearooms of London for the *San Francisco Examiner*. Her other work has appeared in *The Bloomsbury Review, Poets & Writers, SOMA Magazine*, and elsewhere. One of her short stories was selected by the PEN Syndicated Fiction Project and broadcast on N.P.R.'s *The Sound of Writing*.

Blue Circle Press
P.O. Box 460055
San Francisco, CA 94146

ORDER FORM

Quantity	Title	Price
	San Francisco in a Teacup	$15.95 ea.
	Subtotal	
	Shipping (see below)	
	CA residents, add sales tax	
	TOTAL	$

Shipping: $4.00 for first book, $1.00 for each additional book.
Foreign orders, please inquire about rates.
Prices subject to change without notice.

Method of Payment (Please make payable to BLUE CIRCLE PRESS)
❏ Cheque   ❏ Money Order

Thank You!

ORDERED BY

Name _____

Address _____

City _____State_____Zip_____

Phone _____

SHIP TO (if different than above)

Name _____

Address _____

City _____State_____Zip_____

Clip & Send